JULIA CLEMENTS' GIFT BOOK OF FLOWER ARRANGING

JULIA CLEMENTS' GIFT BOOK OF FLOWER ARRANGING

NEWNES BOOKS
LONDON · NEW YORK · SYDNEY · TORONTO

CONTENTS

First published in 1969 for Newnes Books by
The Hamlyn Publishing Group Limited,
London · New York · Sydney · Toronto
Astronaut House, Feltham, Middlesex, England

Fifth impression 1975

ISBN 0 600 42143 0

Printed in England by Butler & Tanner Limited, Frome and London

INTRODUCTION

In this book I have endeavoured to present the reader with information on every aspect of the art of flower arranging. It is the result of thousands of requests for such a book from those who are taking their first steps in this fascinating art, and from others, more advanced, who are wondering what their next step should be.

How to answer everyone's questions on flower arranging between one set of covers is a problem which has been much in my mind these last few years. This *Gift Book of Flower Arranging* is the result. I feel confident that tens of thousands of enthusiasts will find the answers to their immediate problems in the pages which follow.

Flower arranging is a vast subject never ending in appeal and it is an interest from which you can seldom turn back for its attraction goes beyond flowers and gardens. It opens your eyes to form, shape and colour. You become drawn by design which helps you assess your home and garden with different eyes. You see magic in a frost-covered branch in winter, or find serenity in a water-lily in summer. You look at glass, china and pottery with the discerning eye of a flower arranger – an eye which makes you want to discover how all these items are created. You will never again walk down a country lane without 'seeing' pieces of wood, fungus, moss, grasses and twigs. They were always there but had previously gone unnoticed; now all these items will help you paint your pictures with flowers. You will 'see' stones and shells on the beach, you will 'feel' colour, and will become impatient to place all these exciting items together.

I have often referred to flower arranging as a therapy, for no matter how big or small our particular problems or worries, the tension is eased the moment we place a few flowers in a container. Of course, you are creating, but by giving yourself over to the flowers the worries seem to float away.

It is for this reason that more and more people are being drawn to this wonderful hobby, for everyone can do it. However, I have not forgotten those who are already well advanced in the skills of flower arranging, and so have enlarged upon certain aspects of the art by including a chapter on 'The Way Ahead'. Sometimes I think we are going too fast, and yet it would be impossible for flower arranging to stand still at a time when everything else about us is changing with a rapidity which is hardly comprehensible.

So, I trust all those who arrange and love flowers will continue to interpret their gentle message to all those who are 'seeing' flowers for the first time.

Julia Clements

TO BEGIN AT THE BEGINNING

BASIC EQUIPMENT

No one can cook without utensils, or paint without brushes - it is the same with flower arranging. To be proficient, you need tools.

You can start simply, with a container (this term covers any receptacle that will hold water), a flower pin-holder, some wire netting and perhaps some flower scissors. Equip yourself with these basic items and add to them as you progress.

In addition to these items, I have a large drawer in which I keep all kinds of gadgets: strips of lead for adding to the back of a tall container to give it weight so that the flowers will not fall forwards; Plasticine for holding dry arrangements and anchoring a pin-holder when necessary; blocks of Oasis or Florapak for transportable arrangements; toothpicks for fixing fruit together; stub wires for giving false stems to cones, dry leaves and other items; candle-cup holders for fixing with Plasticine in the candle-holder part of a candlestick, giving a wider aperture for a flower arrangement; Universal bowl for screwing to a lamp-stand or fixing in a cork to insert in a bottle; bottle-holder, similar to a candle-cup holder but with a long spout enabling it to be inserted in any bottle; thin reel wire for winding several thin stems together and for tying down wire netting in a large container; several tins painted different colours to stand on wooden bases; boxes of marble chips and different-sized pebbles; and a cupboard for pieces of drift-wood, and perhaps another for storing different kinds of bases, with shelves above holding containers and accessories. Although not all of this is necessary in the beginning, you see how far you can go!

Sprays of Grevillea asplenifolia *are here tucked into the opening of a pottery jar and give sufficient support to three short-stemmed yellow tulips in this design for a beginner. The jar stands on a green velvet-covered cardboard cake stand*

Special flower scissors can be bought from horticultural suppliers. They are not expensive and will prove to be a good investment. They will cut most twigs and heavy stems and are invaluable for cutting wire netting for the insides of containers. With care, these scissors will last a long time, and although you may think you can manage with ordinary scissors (which only squash the stems of your flowers) you will find many occasions when only flower scissors with their saw-edge will do.

Stub wires are obtainable in various thicknesses, but an amateur flower arranger seldom needs anything more than gauge 22. The wires are used mainly for giving false stems to dry leaves and cones and for supporting broken or bent stems. When using fresh flowers, however, the use of wires is frowned upon, especially in show work.

Whilst many manage to do all their flower arranging in the kitchen or on an odd table somewhere, other keen arrangers have made flower rooms in attics, disused garages or any spare room in the house, sometimes even investing in a shed or lean-to greenhouse. So with all this advice in mind, equip yourself well.

I am sure you are already anxious to start making a flower arrangement, but be patient. As this chapter is for beginners I want to put down all the information I can.

CONTAINERS

Today almost any receptacle that will hold water for flowers is termed a container. Wineglasses, goblets, copper kettles, bottles, tins, baskets, converted lamp-stands, formal flower vases, fruit dishes and cake stands, jugs, basins, bowls, dishes and ovenware, as well as fine china and silver items are all introduced to play their particular role in the ultimate design. Tall, upright vases are generally accepted as being the better choice for formal arrangements, whilst the shallow dish type of container is more suitable for the modern style. Small containers such as wineglasses are ideal for small flowers; it is most important to suit the flowers to their containers. Suiting flowers to containers is a particular facet of flower arranging.

HOLDERS

Holders are very important, for it is almost impossible to make a well-designed picture with flowers unless you use some kind of holder to keep the flowers firmly in place. For upright vases a piece of crumpled wire netting gives excellent support, provided you push it well down into the vase.

Short ragged ends can be tucked over the rim of the vase to keep the wire steady, or you can tie it down with a piece of your reel wire, with string, or even an elastic band. Wire netting can be obtained in most household stores where you can buy it by the yard, or you can obtain it in some florists' or departmental stores. A 2-inch mesh is the best for general use though you may need a finer mesh for small flowers.

The wire should be cut according to the size and shape of your container. If you mean to fill the vase, it is best to have the wire twice the width and twice the height. It takes a little time to fix the wire netting firmly in the container, but it is time well spent. Do see that it reaches *just above the rim* of the container, and do not crumple it too tightly, making sure you have a fair amount of space in the centre where most of the stems will meet. Once the wire is fixed and assumes the shape of a particular container, it is better to leave it permanently in place. Changing it to fit another container will give you a lot of trouble. It is better to have wire netting ready-fitted to each of the containers you might use.

I often use a pin-holder under wire netting, and can get the best and quickest results in this way. This method is particularly good for a tall, wide opening in a container like a compote stand, for the stems placed vertically down through the wire on to the pin-holder will be held firm, whilst others can be inserted almost horizontally through the wire at the sides and front. I use this method also in a shallow cake tin which I often stand on a silver or white china cake stand.

Flower pin-holders are essential. They are made in many sizes and shapes and are used mainly in shallow dishes for modern designs. They appear as a number of closely-packed nails held point upwards in a heavy lead base, and can be obtained at most florists or stores. Very heavy holders containing larger nails can be obtained for holding weighty branches while a Wonder pin-holder has very fine sharp pins for all flowers and foliage, especially thin-stemmed flowers such as sweet peas and freesias. By selecting the right pin-holder, almost all flowers are easily fixed in the pattern you wish.

If you find your pin-holder is inclined to topple, try fixing it firmly to the base of the container with Plasticine. Press three round knobs of Plasticine on to the dry base of the holder, then press it down on to the dry surface of the base of the dish, giving it a twist as you do so. As you progress you should not need Plasticine because if your design is well balanced it will not topple, but, in the beginning, you may as well save yourself frustration!

Pin-holders are also useful in some tall containers - the sort which are so tall that flowers placed in them fall to the bottom and only the heads are seen! You can overcome this trouble by more than half-filling the container with sand or wet newspaper and then placing a pin-holder on this false surface.

Pin-holders and wire can be seen easily in clear-glass containers and don't look very attractive. As alternatives try using a small roll of crumpled wire netting at the top of the opening of the vase, or try criss-crossing the top with clear Sellotape, inserting the flowers in the openings. Leaves can always be trailed over the rim to hide either of the contrived aids.

Oasis and Florapak are plastic substances which hold water and allow you to move your flower arrangement without fear of it coming to pieces or spilling water. They are ideal for show work and for a special party

Here some vases and equipment are shown. The metal cone seen in the uppermost vase gives added height to a tall arrangement. Also shown is a shallow container for modern design and a shell container, plus pin-holders, wire netting, stub wires, Oasis, candle-cup holder, flower scissors and reel wire

occasion, though I only use these in an emergency for one piece cannot be used many times. They should be steeped in water for some hours then placed in the container and the flowers inserted. Water can be added each day and it has the great advantage that you can place your flowers at any angle, even

Here a number of trivet stands are shown upon which can be stood a bowl. Also shown are a modern container (centre), some fine pin-holders and a candle pin-holder

pointing downwards, and they will still be held and able to absorb moisture.

BASES

Bases are an important part of flower arranging. Not only do they preserve the surface of furniture on which the flower arrangement stands, but they can add colour, atmosphere and even balance to many designs. A shiny black, wooden base placed under a tall, matt white container will not only help balance the flowers in the container but will give interest to the whole design.

Not many bases can be bought, though some are appearing in the shops and at flower shows, but they can easily be made. Slices of wood can be rubbed with linseed oil and pumice powder; other pieces of wood obtained in the household stores can be painted any colour. Rubber door stops screwed to the underside of a large square of wood make an effective base which can then be painted, and a curved slab of wood rubbed over with grate polish will make your base look like antique pewter. There is no end to the style and the use of bases, and as you progress you will never have enough of them, for whether they are round, square, oblong or curved, there will always be an occasion when one of them is just right.

BASIC PATTERNS OF ARRANGING

Is it the flowers or the vase, the occasion or the setting, which inspires you to begin a flower arrangement? I am often asked this question. Of course, the answer is that it is a little of each, although in home decoration, the setting is really the guiding factor.

For instance, if you want flowers placed beneath a lamp on a small table, you will need a small container and delicate flowers, perhaps arranged in a low design, because the lamp is tall. If, however, you wish for flowers placed in the centre of a side table backed by a wall, you will need to make a triangular arrangement of larger flowers. Alternatively,

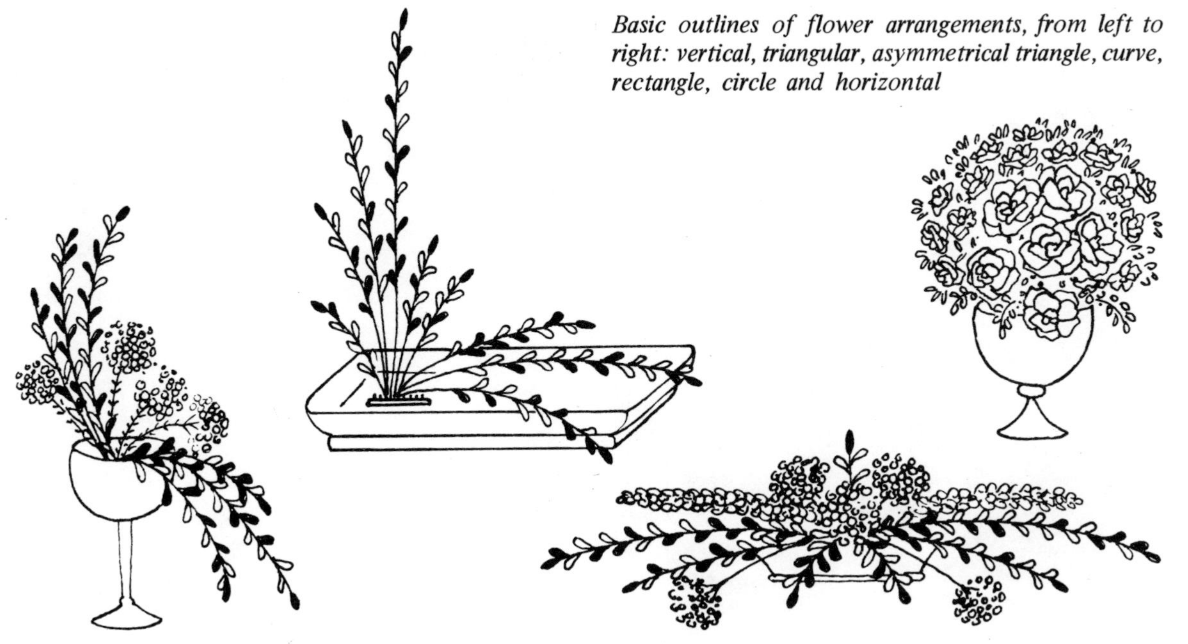

Basic outlines of flower arrangements, from left to right: vertical, triangular, asymmetrical triangle, curve, rectangle, circle and horizontal

(Above) These small flowers, white freesias, blue muscari and short stems of pale green Helleborus corsicus *are perfectly scaled to the delicate Victorian china hand vase*

(Left) This vertical design of chrysanthemums and bulrushes is suitable for a narrow ledge in a corner. The base gives it stability. Small palmetto leaves backed the flowers

you might prefer to place flowers one end of a mantel shelf, in which case you would make an asymmetrically designed arrangement of flowers which more easily flow or trail downwards.

I will deal with colour later in the chapter, but first I suggest that you concentrate on one or other of the basic designs.

Many people dislike the introduction of basic patterns or geometrical designs, but even so I have discovered that these same people often started flower arranging in this way. Of course as you progress you do not necessarily need to follow a pattern, but if you want inspiration at first, you must have a starting point, and a pattern is a great help.

For the sake of having something to fall back on when in doubt, the basic patterns are: vertical; triangular; asymmetrical triangle; curve, sometimes called the Hogarth curve; horizontal; rectangle and circle. I have tried to show you each one in the sketches.

All these patterns will have their uses in different circumstances. A tall, vertical arrangement would be ideal for a narrow ledge in a corner, whereas a horizontal shape would be better for a dining-table. As you progress you will recognise these shapes and their uses, and later on, when these patterns are automatically registered in your mind, you may even manage without them. They will still be there and you will use them in a subtle manner, but you will not think about it. With practice you will know naturally what to do, leaving your mind free for creation and to express something of yourself in your arrangement.

So if you want to be an artist with flowers do not be afraid to make a start. Never be intimidated by wondering what others might think. Be yourself: make a grouping now and allow your picture to be your very own. It is *your* creation and until you wish to learn more, or try something different, your first picture should give you tremendous satisfaction.

THE TECHNICAL TERMS

In the beginning, I advise you not to pay too much attention to principles and technical terms, for although a knowledge of them will finally take you further along the road to success, they really belong to the middle of your study. At first you need to *do* something, anything, as long as you start.

Later on, if you wish to become a really expressive arranger, comes the study of such principles as design, balance, scale, rhythm, transition, texture, colour, composition, line and focal points. This period, while meant as a time of improvement, often holds the arranger back, for she is then more concerned with technicalities than with the development of her own ideas. Later, when these technicalities have become second nature to her, she will find herself able to branch out on her own, and to reject this cramping adherence to principles. They are still there of course, but they are now so automatic that although the artist is constantly guided by them, she works without being aware of them. So let us look at them as they apply to flower arrangements.

Design

This is the structural pattern of the arrangement; it decides the shape, height or width and consists of a planned relationship between the flowers, leaves, container and location in the room.

Any design can be produced to suit any occasion, but some of the most accepted designs used are those variations of the triangle, rectangle, oval, circle, vertical irregular triangle, crescent and low half-circle.

No grouping of any items can appear integrated or attractive without a feeling for design.

These late summer flowers are held in a candle-cup holder in a candlestick, while the design illustrates the beauty of rhythm. Swerving stems of wild clematis (old man's beard) were used for the outline, with green tobacco flowers, sorbus berries, veronica and asters filled in the design

Study the following symbols and you will see what I mean.

```
                                       |
                                      |·|
|||| — . . S S . . || —            — · S S · —
                                      |·|
                                       |
```

As they appear first they are just lines and dots, but when re-grouped in accordance with principles of design they make an acceptable pattern. So it is with flowers, plants, leaves and fruit. By placing the tallest and slenderest material, whether it be tall blooms, wood or fine green sprays, on the outside, and the bigger, more dominant items at the focus of attention at the base of the main stems, the eye is led from the outside or top of the design to the hub of interest, where the eye should rest. Design means the joining together of items of different size, form and colour into a unified whole: this co-ordination of stems or items being emphasized by dominant interest.

In flower arrangements dominant interest could be the largest or brightest coloured bloom; with foliage it could be a group of variegated leaves; with fruit it could be the brightest or most shiny piece, and in plant arrangements it could be the largest-leaved plant. Large stones and chunks of wood can also be items of dominant interest in modern arrangements. The spot in the design where the dominant interest is placed is often termed the focal point, the heart or the hub of the design.

Balance This is the grouping of plant materials within the design, so placed to give a feeling of stability. There can be two types of

This modern line arrangement depicts a water scene composed of bulrushes, water plants and water lilies. The model heron gives spirit to the 'scene'

balance - symmetric and asymmetric. In the former, if you draw an imaginary line down through the centre of the vase, both sides of the arrangement appear equal, and are usually made with similar material, but in the latter the two sides can be distinctly different and yet have equal visual weight. For instance, a long swerve of fine material, such as michaelmas daisies, at the left of a design can be balanced by a shorter placement of heavier material, perhaps of chrysanthemums or leaves, at the right nearer the centre. Greater interest is achieved this way because the sides are not equal, yet they are equally balanced. It is similar to obtaining balance on a see-saw by placing a heavy man at the right near the central axis and a small child on the end at the left.

Scale Scale means proportion. To scale one's decoration to fit the background in which it will be seen is to keep it in proportion with the other items in the room. It means also keeping the plant material in proportion with the container used, as well as scaling the plant items with each other. For instance, it would be incongruous to place lilies of the valley with a large dahlia. Similarly, a large incurved chrysanthemum used as focal interest in a narrow-necked vase would be out of scale, whereas the same bloom placed low in a large round flat plate would be *in* scale. Similarly, fine ferns or carrot leaves, although most decorative, would not appear happily placed with large broad funkia leaves, neither would the fine leaves be ideally suited to a pottery container. Yet these same leaves would combine well with plantain seed spikes in a glass container. A tall *Ficus elastica* (rubber plant) will decorate a corner in a lofty room, whereas a grouping of *Begonia rex* leaves backed perhaps with a tall vine or sansevieria would complement a setting in a lower ceilinged, panelled room. Many a delicate drawing-room might be enhanced with trails of ivy, ruffled ferns or tradescantia. So I advise you to think of your setting when planning your arrangements, choosing them in accordance with the background against which they will be seen.

Rhythm Rhythm is a feeling of motion, and is achieved in flower arrangement by the placement of curving lines and graduating sizes leading towards the centre and on again. These lines are part of the original design and are placed in rhythmic curves before the 'filling in' material is added (see page 20). Rhythm can also be obtained by colour. For instance, you could start at the top with a pale tint of a

these leaves, the centre were finished with delicate leaves or grasses, because the weight would then be in the wrong place. So do open your eyes to the textural value of different flowers, leaves and plants.

Colour

Colour is a vast subject, and is very important in flower arrangements. For years I have been studying colour and its qualities, but I do not think it should be over-emphasized to the student flower arranger. Such casual advice as 'by mixing a little white with a colour a tint can be obtained' can be very confusing, for we must remember that as artists with living plant material we are using nature's gifts and not paints, and nothing we, as arrangers, can do will alter the colour of the plants we group together. The necessary point to know is *where* to place plants of certain colours for best effect either in a design or in a room.

However, before we can talk about colour we must agree on terminology. A TINT is a lighter version of a colour (i.e. lime and apple green are *tints* of green) and tints are generally better used as highlights. They may be introduced in the centre of a design as focal interest, or if used on their own may become the highlight of a dark corner in a room. Similarly a SHADE is a darker version of a colour, so that bottle green is a *shade* of green, and is better used to bring a number of light elements in a room together, or to give depth to a flower, plant or leaf arrangement.

I generally find it better not to distribute my colours evenly, so when faced with a choice I suggest that you either make your design predominantly shaded, introducing a few tints, or use mainly tints, focalising with shades. Obviously there will be variations between these extremes, but in the main it is better to allow one to be subordinate to the other.

Colour affects our senses, so remember that gay and striking effects can be gained by using the warm colours, such as red, yellow, and orange, whilst more soothing and delicate effects can be obtained by using blue-pinks, mauves, blue, purple and grey foliage. (I have referred again to the question of colour in chapter nine.)

Composition

Every flower, leaf or plant arrangement is in itself a composition, although in show schedules this word is generally taken to include accessories. So many novices wonder how to begin composing a flower arrangement. The secret of composing is to bring together a number of elements in a rhythmic movement that finishes on a pleasing note: so when setting out to make a composition collect all your items and decide which of them shall be used for *main interest,* because everything you want to express with them cannot be of equal importance. If therefore you have picked onion seedheads and artichoke heads for the centre, it would be better to eliminate one of them, just as you must decide between bright green peppers and pale yellow lemons for main interest in a grouping of fruit, because the rest of the composition must be subordinate to one dominant interest only.

Of course this will be much simpler if you can decide what you want before picking or buying. Suppose that when looking for leaves in the garden for a flowerless design you find some flushed green megasea leaves which you think will be ideal for central interest: you will then look for some different shapes to go behind them, finally searching for fine sprays for the outside. In a smaller garden you might find a twisted branch to give height to a modern design, and use the megasea leaves for

Five natural-coloured cycas leaves formed the modern outline for the three protea blooms. Root-wood gave added interest and covered the pin-holder dish

transition to your main interest, which could be apples, cones, or a piece of tree wood.

Focal point

This is sometimes termed the 'target', 'highlight', 'heart' or 'the accent' of the design: it is the centre of interest in an arrangement. It is the point in the design where all the stems unite, and the place where the most important material should be placed. Important, I mean, either for size, colour, dominance or texture.

Line

Line is the passage on which your eye is led from one item to another in the arrangement. Each bud, leaf or flower, by its size or colour should be so placed as to take your eye from a starting point to the central point of interest where it should rest. If you remove all colour from a flower arrangement, such as unfortunately happens in a black-and-white photograph, an arrangement with good line should still emerge successfully from this acid test.

FLOWER AND FOLIAGE FORMS

The most repeated difficulty I have met during my constant travels to talk to the novice flower arranger, has been how to convey the meaning of such a vast subject as flower arranging in the short space of one afternoon or evening.

I finally developed a theory to prove that, if different forms of material were used in the correct placements according to three basic principles, anyone, and I really mean *anyone*, could make a flower arrangement.

I found that an audience was not helped very much by watching lovely and intricate arrangements made by an expert. They were entertained, yes, and full of admiration for all they saw, but they either had no similar material to use themselves, or they did not know why it had been used, and so little advance was made.

I wanted to make my students *feel*. I wanted them to say, 'Why, I could do that'. I finally preferred working to some simple rules that would give novices encouragement and evoke their *own* ideas rather than making elaborate designs myself, for it is the sense of personal achievement in creating a simple design that thrills a novice and urges her to attempt more ambitious arrangements later. Most teachers develop their own approach to students and I do not presume that all agree with me, but in order to help those who are continuing the good work of helping others, I repeat that my simplified theory is to remember three moves: (1) the outline or design, (2) filling in, (3) the focal interest; and in order to translate these moves effectively, material of different sizes and forms should be employed.

For instance, *Type A (Points)*: tall, fine, pointed material *for the outline. Type B (Fillers)*: shorter, rounder and spray material *for filling in. Type C (Dominants)*: larger and heavier textured blooms, deep or dominant colours, anything to give visual weight for *focal interest.*

Under the heading of Points (Type A) would come such flowers as delphiniums, lythrum, antirrhinums, gladioli and golden rod. Pointed foliage such as the leaves of flax, privet, gladiolus, iris, artichoke, carnation and grevillea would also be included in Type A material, just as would slim branches of forsythia, yew, pussy willow, and the like. Fine grasses, bare branches and buds all come in this category, and when you are accustomed to design you will appreciate that these points are so placed on the outside of the design, so as not to hold your interest. This pointed material should lead your eye to the centre of the arrangement, where it should be held by the more important material.

Type B or Filler material, as I call it, can include such flowers as sweet williams, marguerites, spray chrysanthemums, scabiosa, sweet peas and many others. Certain leaves could be included here, in fact any material that is broader than Type A is suitable for these secondary placements.

Type C or Dominant material can include most of the larger round flowers, or those which are arresting because of their peculiar shape or variety. Roses, which are often termed the queen of flowers, are good Type C material, for they demand to be seen in a prominent place. Paeonies, rhododendrons and large clusters of smaller flowers come under Type C heading; also any large leaves such as magnolia, laurel, paeony, kale, rhododendron and others.

Clusters of berries and fruit are also Type C, and do remember that material of white, pale pink and pale yellow can be as dominant in a design as the most carefully chosen deep-coloured material. It is both the size and importance that count.

Materials which are prominent, important or heavier in texture are used as focal interest because they give visual weight at this point where all the other spreading stems should unite. In other words, all the material should appear to spring from this unifying weight, or, conversely, if you contemplate the outside of the design first, the points should lead your eye to it. Please do not think that just one large flower will give the best focal interest. Try to make this area arresting by subtle placements. Five flowers of varying sizes might be more interesting; three flowers surrounded by leaves might prove an excellent

The strong texture of the yellow arum lilies combines well with the heavy pottery dish in this modern line design. Lichen-covered twigs give height and mahonia leaves surround the pin-holder on which the material is held

solution; a rosette of rhododendron leaves, from the centre of which might spring some berries, would be quite effective.

In other words, try to avoid placing an obvious blob in the centre; aim at interest through subtlety. As you progress in your study and appreciation of the finer points, you will perhaps do without focal interest altogether, although by the fact that you have correctly placed your stems it will be there.

When you review this short reference to flower forms, you will realise how easy it is to make an effective flower arrangement. In fact, at the risk of being called assertive, I would urge those of you who are beginners to repeat quite often to yourself these words: outline, fill in, focal point, using points, fillers, and dominants, in the order of tall, shorter, short.

You can translate these moves with a mass of assorted material, or in a shallow plate you could use a bare branch for tall line, some leaves for filling in, and a pine cone or a large flower for low interest.

I have repeatedly pointed out that it is only after these moves become automatic in thought and execution that your mind is left free for creation. It is then that the real joy of this expressive art commences, for with mental freedom you can then make an arrangement in a certain manner because you feel like it. You will express your personal desires without having to stop and ask yourself where to place the material.

CARE OF CUT FLOWERS

All flowers and leaves need attention if they are to give of their best when cut, so in answer to the cry of how to make them last longer I give a list of some suggestions which I have found most useful, remembering that much depends upon when, and under what conditions, the flowers are bought or picked.

1. Always pick your flowers before they are fully mature.
2. Try to pick flowers at night or early morning when transpiration is at its lowest.
3. Strip off the lower leaves, re-cut the stem ends under water - to avoid an air lock - and leave for some hours in deep water in a dark place before arranging. This treatment will harden and fully charge the stems with water.
4. All woody-stemmed flowers, such as lilac, viburnums, chrysanthemums, roses and other flowering shrubs, should have some of the leaves removed and the stem ends split before being placed in deep water.
5. Leaves and sprays of greenery should be submerged in water for some hours before being used because this will make them strong. In spring and early summer it is best to place young leaves in a bath of water overnight before using them. This does not apply to hairy, 'woolly' leaves such as *Stachys lanata,* for these soak up water like a sponge.
6. Always remove the white portion of the stem ends of bulbous flowers as they drink only from the green portion.
7. Hold stem ends of daffodils, narcissi and similar flowers under warm running water to remove the sticky substance they exude.
8. Tulips will always twist and turn towards the light. Wrap them up to their heads in newspaper and leave overnight in deep water. They then should have taken their stand.
9. Certain flowers, such as delphiniums and lupins, will benefit if the hollow stems are filled with water after cutting, then plugged with cotton wool before being left overnight in deep water to be conditioned.
10. Lupins are best picked when only the

Here flame-coloured gladioli and carnations are arranged in a rectangular pattern on a black base. Pale-green grapes are added low down and hosta lily leaves give weight at the left

three lower rings of florets are open. The stems should be cut straight across, not on a slant, and treated as instructed above.

11. If flowers sent through the post arrive looking rather wilted, re-cut the stem ends and place in very hot water. Soft-stemmed flowers, such as tulips, should not be given this treatment.

12. Wild flowers, picked to take home, should be wrapped in wet newspaper or polythene for the journey; the stems should be re-cut and placed in deep water for some hours or overnight on reaching home.

Root wood screwed to wood base around which modern arrangements are made

13. Always have warm water in the container before starting your arrangement as this prevents the stem ends from drying. A tablet of charcoal in the water will keep it pure. Top up with warm water every day.

14. Sugar in the water will help most flowers to last, with the exception of daffodils and narcissi which exude a sticky substance. Use two teaspoonsful to a pint of water.

15. Roses last longer if the lower leaves and thorns are removed and the stem ends split before placing in water. Wilting roses, left out of water or arriving by post, should have the same treatment but be placed in near boiling water to which a teaspoonful of sugar has been added, and left until revived.

16. Gourds, which form the basis of many dried arrangements, should be picked when fully ripe and the skins are hard, then be placed on newspaper in a warm room or cupboard and wiped frequently to remove transpiration.

17. Mimosa will last longer if stem ends are split and placed in three inches of near-boiling water with a teaspoonful of sugar. Later fill up with warm water and arrange.

18. *Begonia rex* and other rather soft hothouse leaves, if cut and used in decoration, should first be submerged for some hours in water with a spoonful of sugar added.

19. Dahlias, poppies, euphorbia and other flowers that exude a white substance, last longer if the cut stem ends are first stood in two inches of very hot water for about ten seconds. This disperses the substance and allows the warm water in the vase to be absorbed.

20. Blossoming sprays can be forced into bloom by first submerging them in warm water to swell the buds, then, after splitting the stem ends, standing them in warm water in a warm room. Pick the sprays only when the buds are swollen.

21. Camellia, rhododendron, laurel and other large-surfaced leaves look better if they are

wiped over occasionally with a damp, oily rag.

Try experimenting yourself with any items I have not mentioned, but remember that all flower stems should be re-cut and left in deep water for some hours before using. Most leaves should be submerged for some time before use. Woody stems should be split. Have warm water in the vase before starting your arrangement and do not forget to top up with water each day.

MODERN LINE ARRANGEMENTS

There are many different styles in flower arrangement, and having learned the essential background, you can now begin to explore the scope before you. The styles in most frequent use are modern, mass, period, free style, miniature, informal and Japanese. From these styles there are a number of variations - table, sideboard, windowsill, mantel shelf, hall, interpretative, and other show arrangements.

This means you can make a modern table arrangement or a mass table arrangement, or even a period table arrangement, or a 'table' arrangement in any of the other styles. You can also create a hall arrangement in the modern style or the mass style or any other style. In other words there is no set method of making a hall arrangement, for 'hall' is not the operative word. You make a hall arrangement, in a chosen style.

Of all these designs, in this introductory chapter I shall discuss modern line arrangements, mass and table arrangements. But the basic principles of modern and mass arrangements may be used whether you make your arrangement for a hall, a show or a table.

The modern style is suitable for all contemporary settings - new flats, offices, or housing estates. Most modern designs are made in shallow dishes, using a large pinholder to hold the flowers in place. Others are made in tall, upright or angular containers. You will find that they all show in common a strong line, strong form and strong colour.

The most arresting modern designs show three changes in form with a fourth added - if the arranger is clever. This means you use tall, strong height, perhaps a bare branch; some large, bold leaves such as *Fatsia japonica,* castor-oil plant, funkia, bergenia or magnolia and some vibrant-coloured flowers. In other words, you place together three strong forms in three strongly opposing colours.

You may not always have these three different forms, although I am sure you will try to obtain them if you want to create good modern designs. However, should the plants not be available, you can still make an exciting design by using strong flowers all of one kind, then adding, low down, a piece of wood, some leaves or even stones.

I am often asked what makes a good modern design, and my own belief is that line is of the greatest importance.

There must be a strong linear pattern - a good silhouette. The effect must be uncluttered, and this means not putting in too much or using too many kinds of flowers. The forms and colours should be bold. Although mauve flowers can be made into a modern line, they are not the best choice for a modern design.

Choose the vibrant colours such as orange, scarlet and yellow. Use large green leaves, big chunks of wood, large white stones, big chunky containers. Try to get the feel of the wood and you will be successful. For instance, certain flowers seem to be more correct for modern designs than others. Gladioli, anthuriums, dahlias, oriental poppies, all seem suitable, whereas sweet peas, delphiniums, roses, and others would appear better in more formal arrangements.

The more you look at and try to analyse the flower arrangements you see, the more you will appreciate these principles. Of course, all those you see will not always depict the basic teaching but you can learn from them, even if only what to avoid.

Do not underestimate your own judgement of flower arrangement. Speak up to any critics. Ask questions and discuss or even argue the subject. In this way you will learn.

A modern design can be upright, made in a vertical or rectangular line, or it can be 'free' style - a line you have made up yourself. But in every case try to see that it is balanced, each side being visually equal, and make sure it is in proportion to the setting.

If you would like to start by making a *rectangular* design, see that your tallest stem is not less than one-and-a-half-times the length of your low container. I nearly always have my first stem twice the length of the container, but this may appear too bold if you are just beginning. Place your pin-holder one end of the container, let us say at the left, and insert this tall stem about two-thirds to the back of the holder. This will leave you room for the rest of the material which has to be added.

Now cut the next stem to a length which is two-thirds that of the first one, and place it leaning back slightly at the left of the main stem.

The third stem can be cut one-third the height of the first one, and can be placed low to the right, pointing forward slightly even if it protrudes over the rim. All the main stems should appear to spring from the same point.

Next, you can cover these three lines with further flowers, or you can add some leaves, placing more at the left. And remember, if you are to get good balance, you will draw your imaginary line down through the tallest stem, and as you placed the holder at the left of the container you now have quite a lot of visual weight in the part of the container showing at the right. More leaves at the left will help to balance this. You could use rhododendron or laurel leaves, kale or bergenia, but not thin, spiky leaves, for you have already used tall, thin items for the outline.

Easy, isn't it? These lines are only given as a start. You can vary them if you like, perhaps by placing the tallest at the right and the shortest flowing out low at the left, or placing the tallest first and the shortest next, with the medium-length stem flowing out low down. There is no set rule, but when beginning it is better to follow a principle until you are confident enough to ignore it.

Modern designs are also created in upright containers, such as tubular, box-like and angular types. You can follow the same principle, using stems one-and-a-half-times the height of the container, and you can vary the previous design by making a vertical line, placing flowers one below the other, finishing with some leaves near the rim.

Wood, stones, cones, gourds, fruit and ornaments are all assets in modern designs. A modern design can be created around an ornament, in which case the ornament becomes the focal interest, providing it is dominant enough. Tall height is placed behind it and shorter flowers or leaves can be inserted behind and in front. An ornament is termed an 'accessory' in the flower arranger's language.

When using an ornament, it should become an integral part of the design, and should be relative in texture, colour and scale to the rest of the plant material being used. To make this more clear you should never use an ornament *after* making your arrangement, simply because you happen to have one around.

Having read through this simple guide to modern line arrangements, you might like to try one for yourself. Make a modern freestyle design by placing a pin-holder at the left of a shallow dish and inserting a tall, swerving branch. Angle this to swerve across the dish to the right and upwards. Then low down, near the holder, add some leaves and three flowers. Fill the dish with water.

MASS ARRANGEMENTS

There are probably no greater exponents in the art of making mass flower arrangements than the British. It may be because such an abundant variety of flowers and other plant material grows here. It may also be because a mass arrangement of flowers stands out on its own, and can even compete, as it has done so admirably for generations, with the lavish backgrounds, art treasures and pictures that are found in our great houses.

For this reason, in the flower arranging world, a mass arrangement is often termed *le bouquet anglais* and yet many beginners ask: 'What is a mass arrangement?'

It means just that: a mass. It is a collection of flowers making a compact form. Of course, years ago, flowers of all one kind were picked from the garden and were massed into a large vase. They were enjoyed for their colour, their perfume or for their horticultural perfection. Today, modern mass arrangements are still composed of a collection of flowers and leaves, but more attention is paid to the planning of the arrangement, with more knowledge of colour distribution, and the flowers are placed much more loosely and with greater natural flow, so that each bloom can be seen.

But do not imagine that line is not introduced into mass arrangements - it is. Whereas in modern designs the line is uncluttered and boldly silhouetted, the line in mass arrangements is covered up by more plant material. Nevertheless, even in mass arrangements, all the lines should meet at the focal point and should appear to flow from it. There should be 'transition' in a mass arrangement - the placement of flowers each shorter than the other, so that the eye moves slowly, without sudden jarring, from the top to the base of the arrangement and from the outside to the centre.

When an ornament is used it should be in keeping with the flower design. Here you see an oriental figurine complementing the pale-pink chrysanthemums placed at the base of tall red cornus shrub stems

There are many methods of making a mass arrangement of flowers. Some start by placing the focal interest first and then build up and around it, but I prefer to establish the height and the width of the arrangement first, then to work down from the top to the centre, and in from the outside to the centre.

First fill the container with crumpled wire netting or, if using some heavy flowers, try placing a pin-holder underneath the wire

netting. Tie the wire down to the container or bend the ends of the wire over the rim to keep it firm whilst working. Make sure the wire comes to just above the rim of the container, for this will allow you to make flowing outward swerves. If the wire is below the rim, your arrangement will finish up rather stiff and upright.

Make the outline of your design by using the tallest and finest stems at least one-and-a-half-times the height of the container. Make sure that your tallest stem is placed very firmly, for it is around this that the rest of the arrangement is composed. Place it down through the wire and on to the pin-holder starting two-thirds to the back of the container. This will leave you room in front for filling in and a little space at the back for adding leaves to give the finishing touch. The side stems can be two-thirds as long as the tallest.

Next, insert some larger flowers down the centre, making the lower ones point forward over the rim. At this stage you can also add some larger leaves around the centre, emphasising the central interest. This also gives a feeling of stability and covers up some of an apparently frightening mass of empty wire netting.

Finally, fill in by working slowly down from the top to the centre, and in from the outside to the centre, with less important flowers, placing some so that they tilt forward. Insert others closer in, near the wire, giving a third-dimensional effect. Make sure that a few of the low flowers are placed almost horizontally at the side and in front, for some should appear to flow forward over the rim.

This triangular mass arrangement is composed of pale-pink and mauve larkspur on the outside with roses in the centre. Astilbes, pinks and nigella helped to fill in the design

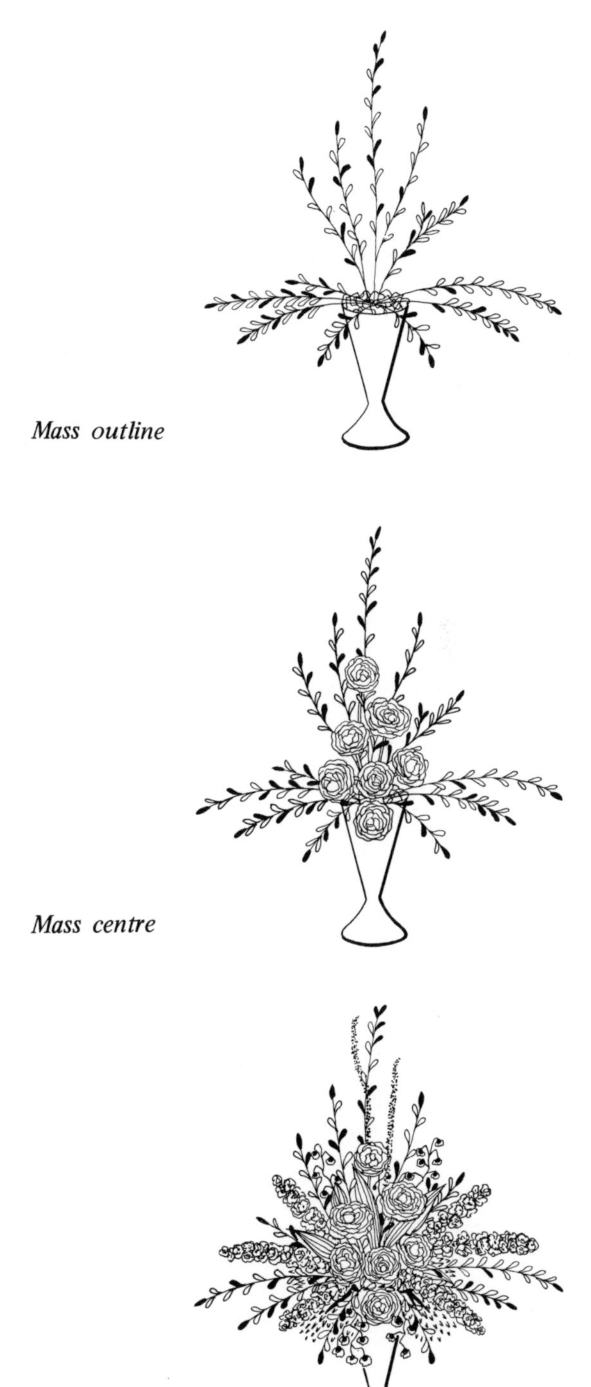

Mass outline

Mass centre

Mass fill-in

If you are making a mass arrangement entirely from one kind of flower such as paeonies, gladioli, iris or chrysanthemums, you should follow the same method, but try to use some fine foliage to give the outline, adding larger leaves around the centre for emphasis. The flowers should be cut to varying lengths and a number of them *recessed* or placed *in,* near to the wire. This gives them a smaller appearance than those which point forward. In this way, even with only one kind of flower and no leaves, you can obtain the effect of some flowers being smaller and some larger by placing them 'in' and 'out'.

Leaves are particularly important in mass arrangements because they give depth and a change of form, so even if your garden is small I would advise you to concentrate on growing some leaves. If you do not possess a garden, a florist will be able to supply you with some, and better still, a walk in the country once a week will reveal untold treasures.

The colouring in a mass arrangement can be according to your own personal wish. It may be that you want to make a harmonious colour scheme of garden flowers. In this case it is better to pick only those colours which are near to each other on the colour wheel - in other words, analogous colours - or all the tints and shades of one colour, making a monochromatic scheme. I have explained these terms under the heading on colour on page 190. Whether you make your focal point of a dark colour or a light colour depends upon the size of the flowers. Pale pink paeonies would be ideal for focal interest, but pale pink sweet peas would not, because they are not strong enough. A dark crimson paeony would also be ideal in the centre, but dark antirrhinums would not. Do not, however, make the focal point obvious. I have seen many arrangements quite delicately made, containing in the centre a large dark flower which, the arranger explained, was the focal point. The focal point should be there in your mind. It can be emphasised with some leaves or berries or the most important flowers can be placed there, but do not just add one for the purpose - it will only jar and look completely out of place.

When using dark, pointed flowers for the outside of a design try to add some lighter foliage behind them or near them to help them show up in greater relief or, alternatively, place them near a pale background.

Mass arrangements can be made in any style you like - mass tables, mass sideboards, mass triangles, and so on - but in every case all the lines of the stems, whether naturally curved branches, flowers or leaves, should appear to meet at a point underneath the tallest stem.

TABLE ARRANGEMENTS

Almost everyone longs to be able to make attractive table arrangements. Perhaps this is because a home possesses so many ideal settings for flowers. There is the hall table, the lounge table and the dining-room table, as well as small coffee tables, all of which can be attractively decorated with flowers.

Most other designs are termed 'frontal' arrangements, since they are mainly seen from the front, although even these arrangements should be made to be viewed from front and sides as well. Table arrangements, on the other hand, are usually made to be viewed all round, so although you can follow most of the principles I have already explained, I feel sure you will find it easier if, at the beginning, you try one of my teaching principles. There are many ways of making a table arrangement and I shall discuss these later, but first of all,

The main line in this asymmetrical arrangement is off-centre which allows for a longer swerve low at the right. The colour scheme here was cream, beige, tan and brown. All the material was held by wire netting in a gilt container

try starting with just thirteen fine stems.

As a container, you can use an oblong baking tin, perhaps painted an attractive colour, or you can use a low bowl or tureen. Fill the container with crumpled wire netting, or, if you prefer, wire netting over a pin-holder. Make sure you are planning your arrangement suitably to the size of the table. As a guide, you might like to make the arrangement one-sixth the surface area of the table, although, if a meal is planned, much will depend upon the other items on the table.

Having filled the container with wire, insert five stems, as in the diagram, using pointed plant material. This can be privet, rosemary, lavender, antirrhinums, or any flowers that are not round and dominant.

Insert four shorter stems almost horizontally each side of the third and fifth stems, another tilting forward below the first stem, and another below this, flowing forward over the rim. Repeat these last two on the reverse side. This more or less completes your outline, although to obtain a really light effect, I always add another shorter stem each side, tilting forward between the first and seventh stems and the first and ninth. These last two are repeated on the reverse side.

This gives you a light, airy arrangement which now needs only to be filled in with rounder flowers and leaves, the flowers being placed in between each pointed flower, and the leaves tucked in around the centre to draw all the stems together. Be sure that a few of the lower flowers and leaves flow out over the rim of the container and try to place some of the flowers in near the wire and some projecting out. This avoids a flat effect.

Many people ask if a table arrangement has to be made according to a set height, and although there are no rules laid down, I feel it is better not to make the centre of a home decoration too tall. If it is for the dining table, the family and guests will want to be able to see each other across it! On the other hand, at many official banquets, the flowers are arranged on tall, candelabra-type containers, enabling guests to converse under and in between the flowers.

On many occasions I have made a modern design for a table decoration using a tall, twisty branch for height with a cluster of flowers low down. The tall branch, being fine, does not obstruct anyone's view, and it does prove that much depends on the circumstances. There is no set rule.

You might also like to try building up a 'scene' - something I love to do. You can make a water scene with a few flowers one side of a dish, or with a shallow dish filled with stones and a few woodland flowers and an ornament added. You might even use a pottery cockerel, adding wheat and fruit. All of these scenes can be made to appear equally pleasing when viewed from any angle and they often assume the role of a conversation piece.

Fruit arrangements are particularly ideal for family gatherings. You might enjoy grouping several kinds of fruit on a tray or a bamboo base, adding a few colourful flowers in tubes of water. Fruit can be made to stand firm in a tray by placing it on rubber jar rings, and can easily be fixed together with toothpicks.

You might also like to try an all-foliage table arrangement. These can be made very quickly - particularly useful when unexpected guests arrive! I keep a large box of white stones picked up on the sea-shore, as they give excellent contrast and interest when placed between short heads of rhododendron leaves in a shallow bowl. Try green leaves and oranges, but do wash or wipe the dust off large leaves before using them on the table, and they will look much more shiny and attractive.

Buffet tables are also of interest to table arrangers, and although it is generally agreed

This low table design was made with pink larkspur and pinks, with pale-green leaves 'recessed' near the wire. Pale pink candles could be stood each side of the flowers on the table

Table diagram

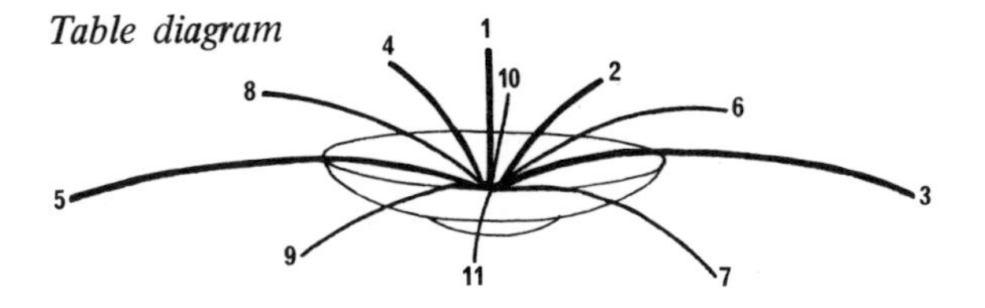

that buffet table arrangements are made fairly high to avoid the flowers getting mixed up with the food on the table, I have also made 'flower trees' each end of a long buffet, adding a short, low decoration in the centre.

However, although the requirements now, of this book, do not include table settings, I do feel that as an interested flower arranger you will enjoy your flowers more if you pay attention to everything on the table, even the cloth. Let suitability be your watchword. Yellow, daisy-like flowers and leaves are ideal set on a brown linen cloth with pottery plates for luncheon, but would not appear nearly as effective placed on a white cloth with white plates for a formal dinner party. Try to look at the scene as a whole and combine the flowers, in colouring, texture and suitability, to everything else on the table.

ARRANGER'S CHOICE

The choice of style for a flower arrangement is endless. The flower arranger can decide on an opulent massed display of fresh summer flowers straight from the garden, or make a simple design with a few precious early spring blooms gleaned from the wood or hedgerows; she can achieve a stark outline with bare branch reminiscent of Japanese thought if that is her mood, or use the tiniest blooms to create an arrangement in miniature. It is the arranger's choice; and in this chapter I have tried to show you in part the wealth of that choice.

MASS STYLE

The formal or classical style of using masses of flowers to gain effect is typically British. Take care that your container blends happily with your room and furniture and remember that the shape of your arrangement should suit its position in the room.

A formal, massed triangular shape is ideal for the centre of a table backed by a wall, whereas an irregularly shaped mass design, i.e. shorter one side than the other, is better for one end of a similar table. A classic mantel vase is most suitable for one or both ends of a mantelshelf; these are usually filled with plenty of flowers, the outsides being made visually heavier and shorter, whilst longer fine trails fall towards the centre and out over the edge of the shelf.

Formal designs call for formal vases, so avoid heavy shallow pottery dishes, so necessary for modern designs, and use instead your formal silver, glass or fine china containers, filled with the more exquisite flowers.

Flowers such as sweet peas, roses, lilies, orchids, delphiniums and the more choice flowers are considered suitable for formal flower arrangements, and colour is also relevant. Mauve, purple, pink, crimson, blue and other delicate colours are all suitable. Small, elegant containers filled with tiny

(Right) This modern scenic design is composed of a tall branch of Mahonia japonica *standing in a well pin-holder behind a piece of rock. Pine and heather are added and the oriental model gives spirit to the composition*

(Page 36) This hall table arrangement is made in an upright classical urn featuring brown iris and brown Prunus pissardii *with white campanulas and white lilies. Yellow* Cytisus battandieri *is seen low at right*

precious flowers and leaves lend an air of formality especially when placed on antique furniture, perhaps under a lamp.

To make a formal triangular arrangement, follow the instructions given in chapter one. First decide where it will finally stand, making the arrangement taller if rooms are high, shorter if low. For large, high rooms use a fairly large vase, for nothing offends the eye more than a large mass of flowers in a small vase.

For an asymmetrical mass formal design, start with the tallest stem off centre at the left, adding large leaves and flowers at the left and longer finer ones low at right.

THE MODERN STYLE

If you live in a house or flat of contemporary design then you will probably be most interested in the modern line style of flower arrangement. Although often appearing more bold and exciting than traditional styles, flower arrangements in the modern manner are, in my opinion, easier to achieve.

To make an original modern design do not be afraid to use strong or contrasting colours; neither must you fear heights, for tall designs are more modern than squat ones. The value of space must be realised, and allowed for round the principal lines of your design: be careful to resist the temptation to fill up the spaces in your arrangement because you are afraid it might appear too sparse.

An appropriate background is most important. If your walls are pale, you can place before them dark branches and bright leaves; if dark it would be better to use striking colours such as yellow, orange and scarlet.

The right container is also a matter for consideration; it should be plain and uncluttered in appearance, perhaps made of thick metal, glass or pottery. It can be shallow or tall depending upon the space to be filled.

Although flowers alone can make interesting modern designs, a contrast of form will make the pattern more eye-catching. For instance, a tall branch with short flowers grouped low down, or tall flowers with a piece of gnarled wood placed low in the design, will prove more exciting than if six flowers all of one kind are placed upright in a container.

So if you are interested in making creative modern arrangements make a start now at looking for those accessories so useful for adding a different shape or form to your design.

Collect some large stones, rough pieces of wood, old roots, dried fungus, shells, even ornaments, for all of these are valuable accessories to modern flower arrangement. Pieces of wood can be sandpapered to obtain interesting textures and other items may be rubbed smooth, polished with shoe polish, and finished in a variety of colours.

TABLE ARRANGEMENTS

It is not easy to generalise when giving suggestions for formal and informal table settings, for there are so many variations. However, it is agreed that when flowers are used on the table, they should be considered as part of the whole setting, and not as an individual flower arrangement. The size of the table, as well as the colour and texture of china, should be taken into consideration, and the table coverings, whether cloths or mats, should all play their part either in accentuating or complementing the colours or theme of the flowers.

(Page 37) Cream and red old shrub roses are here grouped in a china basket suitable for any table

(Left) This mass arrangement of summer garden flowers is made in a low bowl for a side table. Held in wire netting are delphiniums, escallonia, paeonies and Rosa rubrifolia *foliage can be seen*

Flowers for the more formal dinner party, whether small or large, should preferably be of the more precious or fine nature to combine with the best china or glass. Roses, carnations, orchids, freesias and camellias are suitable choices, although those who are gardeners will have a wide choice of personally grown preferences. The flowers can be grouped high round the tops of candelabra, or arranged low in the centre of the table. Variations can take the form of having two small groups at each end of the table, or small arrangements at each place setting, but whatever you choose, colour is important.

If the colouring of the china is not strong (it may be white), the colouring of the flowers can be allowed to dominate; for instance, in autumn, scarlet carnations bursting from a foundation of green hydrangeas, or in spring, orange clivias grouped with green grapes. Freesias with grevillea foliage are also lovely in spring. Camellias add elegance to any table and more particularly if you possess the fine china which features this exquisite bloom.

Water lilies and begonias are favourites for floating arrangements in summer, although the petals of water lilies should be held back while warm candle-wax is poured round the stamens; otherwise they will close up at night. Ivy interwoven with chunks of glass will give a cool effect, while colourful fruit arranged in a sophisticated pyramid pattern will prove very effective at a formal dinner party.

Containers should be elegant and of fine china, glass or silver for the more formal occasion, although a dish similar in pattern to that of the dinner service is often a good choice. Very little of the container is seen, so a shallow glass bowl or a silver cake basket combine with most tableware.

The ideas for arranging flowers on tables are endless, but do remember that they should either be placed high enough so that guests can look under them (as at a banquet), or low enough to be seen over. Candles can give unobtrusive height to a table arrangement - think of colour, size (the flower arrangement can be one-sixth the area of the table) and suitability in relation to the whole setting.

For the less formal occasions, annual garden flowers, such as cornflowers, african daisies, larkspur, pinks and many others, are very suitable and could be in keeping with your less precious china and cutlery. Perennial flowers, such as marguerites, golden rod and michaelmas daisies, can all be successfully featured as decorations for the informal table-setting, especially when they are coupled with containers from the range of those in pewter, pottery, coarse china, chunky glass or wood.

Bright scarlet geraniums in modern pottery containers would be gay and ideal for an alfresco lunch on the terrace, as would a basket of green cabbage leaves with apples and a few yellow flowers. Daffodils fixed on a pinholder in a dish of water standing in a tray full of moss, stones and tree wood would provide a lively picture for an informal spring table-setting, especially if you used a pale apple-green cloth together with wooden-handled cutlery. Flower pots can be washed over with a thick solution of Polyfilla (from the household stores) and be turned into casual plant or flower containers, while all kinds of unusual utensils filled with flowers can be made the centre of attraction for a casual luncheon or dinner table.

ABOUT THE HOUSE

In designing an arrangement, one of the first questions you should ask yourself is 'Where

The mass arrangement of white Campanula persicifolia *and pale-pink paeonies was interspersed with acid-green* Alchemilla mollis *(lady's mantle), while sprays of deeper pink escallonia swerved downwards at the front and back*

will it eventually stand?' The answer to this question will help you to decide on the colour of your flowers, on the shape of your vase and even the style of your arrangement.

Matter of location should in no way interfere with previous advice I have given in this book. It is an additional hint, and I hope that the more you study my suggestions the better will you be able to combine the main essentials so that in time they will become automatic.

If you live in a modern city flat which is decorated in white and red, and wish to take a day in the country in search of material, you would carry in your mind not only the colour scheme of your room, but its size and exactly where your arrangement will finally be placed. You would probably look for red berries to be preserved later and arrange them with bare branches which perhaps you will eventually whitewash. Green leaves would surround the red berries to give a boldness to a design which would be in complete keeping with your interior. Black elderberries would look equally well if arranged with foliage in a stark-white vase, but in your search you would pass by the brown sprays of dried dock, Queen Anne's Lace, ivy bracken, hemlock and grasses, which would not be for you but for the person who wishes to decorate a brown and cream study.

I should like this example to stress the importance of first visualising your picture, for if you can do so it will help you tremendously when planning ahead. Of course, there

(Left) Sprays of flowering Eucalyptus globulus *form the irregular outline to this design of pink carnations and belladonna lilies. Sprays of the* Phytolacca americana *can be seen low right and elsewhere*

(Right) This modern-style design of iris is grouped with primroses at the base, tucked between wood, moss and stone which cover the pin-holder

are times when we must make the best of what we have, but even so the question 'Where will it stand?' will answer a number of your doubts as to how to begin your arrangement.

If you wish to fill a corner in a room with little space for a mass display, try a vertical design placing the accent on the vase.

Mantelshelves need careful thought. Line designs have a special place here if the shelves are modern and narrow. A triangular design is excellent if the flowers are to be the centrepiece of the shelf, whilst a diagonal line should be introduced if the arrangement is to stand at the end.

Massed displays look beautiful if placed on a pedestal in a large room but to enjoy their full beauty they should be viewed from a distance.

All designs for low tables should be made so that you can look down on to and into them. No focal points are required here, but attention should be paid to colour.

It is always advisable to put the finishing touches to your arrangement in the place where it will finally rest so as to allow you a final overall point of view.

MAKING THE MOST OF A FEW

It is not necessary to have a mass of flowers to make a beautiful picture, for each flower is a thing of beauty in itself and if used with imagination this beauty can be brought into your home to become a true expression of your creative self.

The whole art of arranging a few flowers is in the composition, and after a while you will be thrilled to discover so many different ways in which to place one, three, five or more flowers effectively.

With a few flowers your mind has more play, for it is what *you* see in your finished picture that counts. It may be the bold outline of a calla lily that suggests that it should rise in a stately manner from a low base of bold leaves, leaving its bare stem in stark simplicity, or perhaps you feel that five marigolds would look natural if placed in a low vase, informally, just as they grow? The planning of such arrangements is good mental exercise and you will be surprised at the many variations of design that will occur to you.

In this respect I recall with some amusement a club meeting that I attended when I was in the United States of America. I was the speaker, but before I started there was to be, as usual, a ten-minute exercise on flower arrangement. On this occasion the subject was 'Flexibility of Mind' and I was asked to join in. It all sounded so formidable that my reaction was to escape, but as the generous conception of most Americans of our British character was one of dogged persistence, I felt that this was not the time to let the side down. So, with nineteen others, I was let loose in the grounds, told to pick any number up to five leaves or flowers and to arrange them in seven minutes. I felt I was at a strong disadvantage not knowing the extent of the gardens nor what grew in them, so I went straight to a yew tree, picked a small bent branch, which to me represented a quiet place where I would like to sit and think, and then dashed back and placed it in a Chinese-looking boat. The others did much more exciting things, but the real lesson came when each of us was asked to state the reason for our arrangements.

This interlude certainly unloosed a lot of fresh thoughts and I immediately forgot the words I had prepared for the opening of my talk and introduced it with 'Flexibility of Mind'.

I think this proves what fun there is to be had if we open our minds, and on pages 48-50 I have illustrated a few ideas to give you a start. There are hundreds more, but only you can release them and, in so doing, I know you

(Above) In this pink-and-white design for a table anywhere about the house, the tall pink candle is held in a candle pin-holder pressed into Oasis. The miniature white gladioli formed the width which was filled in with pink roses and sprigs of escallonia

(Left) This spring table arrangement is made in the cluster style which features all kinds of short flowers tucked into a mound of wire netting over a bowl

will sense the tremendous satisfaction which comes from creating an original picture with a few flowers.

MINIATURE ARRANGEMENTS

Miniature arrangements are very popular and there is a class for these exquisite pieces at almost every flower show in the country.

To make a miniature arrangement, follow the same principles as for any other flower arrangement. In other words you pay attention to design, good colour combination, the freshness of your flowers, scaling the size of the flowers in proportion to the tiny vase, and, of course, trying to match the flowers in some way to the vase or container. If you can add some little touch of originality so much the better. By that I mean including just that odd, tiny leaf or twist of a sweet pea tendril or some other item, that perhaps would not occur to other people.

Of course, a certain amount of patience is required, but you can always be sure that the perfect detail of miniature arrangements will draw a great deal of admiration from all those who see them.

Usually they measure about 6 inches in height when completed. Some show organisers state they can be larger but, in any case, the measurement is usually stated in the schedule. Of course, at home you can make them what size you like, and although perhaps the greatest fascination is in looking for the tiny flowers and leaves, which are also of considerable botanical interest, you can have a lot of fun searching for unusual containers. All kinds of small receptacles can be brought into use. Thimbles, perfume phials, shells, lipstick-holders, snuff-boxes, walnuts, acorn cups, and lots of items from the children's doll's house will assume importance once you start to consider them.

You can also make interesting containers from Plasticine and carve your own shapes from soap. You can seal the insides of these containers with melted candle wax to make them watertight and paint or varnish the outside to suit your colour scheme. The suitability of the container you use for the flowers is quite important, especially in competitive work. Tiny sprigs of heather will look attractive placed in a walnut shell or on a small piece of bark, whereas miniature roses would appear more lovely bursting from a silver snuff-box or a delicately coloured sea shell.

Making miniature flower arrangements does not mean that you just place some flower buds in a small container backed with a leaf or two. You must really make sure that the flowers and leaves used are all minute in their own sphere and that your miniature arrangement is really a flower composition on a very small scale. In a miniature design, blades of grass can assume the same importance as gladioli leaves in a larger design.

If your miniature arrangement could be enlarged ten times, and still appear perfect in design and scale, then you can be satisfied.

Tiny pieces of broom or the curly ends of old man's beard are good for line and height, whilst the little flowerlets of alyssum and aubrieta and small pieces of Queen Anne's lace all become focal points of interest in a miniature design. Wet sand or Oasis can be used to hold the flowers in place in shallow containers, and rolled-up pieces of fuse wire in the deeper ones. Plasticine will hold dry material in place. Using tiny pieces of dried plant material and a thick mixture of detergent to hold the stems, you might like to make a triangular design in brown and beige colouring, inside a thimble or bottle screw cap. The detergent mixed with water will set firm in a few minutes. Often in the narrow necks of small bottles the material will balance itself and be held firm, but as with most things in flower arranging, a lot of fun lies in experimenting for yourself. I know one

This vertical design of grasses and chrysanthemums is suitable for placing where only a small space is available. Dried gourds finished the design held in a brown tray

enthusiast who has started a collection of miniature containers.

One important tip: do give your flowers a lot of water before placing them, otherwise the heat of your hands on the tiny short stems will make them wilt. Try to make your plan first, then you will not have to handle the flowers too much. I always lay my flowers on a wet cloth while I am doing the arrangement.

When you have finished an arrangement, use Plasticine to fix the vase to a base.

MORE ABOUT CONTAINERS

What is the best type of vase for flower arranging? This question is often asked by the beginner and there is no easy answer because so much depends on so many factors.

In the home, vases should really suit the background. For instance, pewter containers, baskets, or rush mats and wooden bases are ideal for a country cottage, whereas these items used in a period house, such as a Regency-styled home, would appear out of place. Similarly, a beautiful Dresden china container, though lovely in itself, would appear unsuitable for a modern setting.

Most flat dishes, chunky stone jars and wooden bases are ideal for modern-style arrangements, whereas the more elegant silver, fine china or glass-ware type of container is more suitable for a classical background.

In show work the flower arranger has to study the suitability of the container to the flowers being used, in order to interpret the wording of the schedule. The schedule prints the requirements of a show. For instance, if this asks for 'The Bounties of the Country', you know that you can use baskets, wood or

(Left) Only two camellias combined with a branch of hazel catkins prove that it is not how much you use, but how you place a few. The pin-holder which stands at the right of this blue-grey pottery dish was covered with polished stones

(Right) Sprigs of grey centaurea and veronica are here placed with blossom of Viburnum tinus *(laurustinus) to make this gay little winter arrangement*

pewter. If this question arises you must ask yourself why you are making the arrangement, and this will help you to decide on the container.

There is an endless variety of containers in use today, all effective in their right settings, and many which create atmosphere wherever they are placed. The beginner must decide what type of arrangement she wants to make, then find an appropriate container. The department stores today stock a full range. The work of many of the new potters is ideal for modern and Japanese-styled arrangements. Wedgwood and Crown Stafford china have a number of elegant vases in their range, but as a rule, the flower arranger searches for the unusual.

Most lamp-stands can be converted, by the addition of a Universal bowl, into elegant flower containers. These bowls are usually obtainable from florists, can be screwed on to the stand where the bulb would normally be affixed, and are easily transferred from one stand to another. Lamp-stands are inexpensive and carry less purchase tax than vases, so the idea of this extra bowl is worth considering. Another idea is to use a candle-cup fixed in a candlestick.

Tins, no matter what their shape, can also be converted into interesting flower containers. Tall, cylindrical biscuit tins can be painted to look like tubular jars, whilst a square tin can be made to look like an oriental container.

(Above) This tiny china cherub held sprigs of mahonia blossom and single florets of winter jasmine, all placed in Oasis

(Left) Three daffodils placed at the base of stems of pussy willow form an almost crescent-shaped design finished with a little greenery

Smaller tins can be fixed by nails to a flat wooden base, and the whole painted in one colour. When using these tins as containers I varnish them inside to make them watertight, or place a smaller tin inside the larger one which has been pierced by the nail.

I remember once making a container from a square cake tin. I covered the outside with Gesso plaster (you can buy this in the art stores) mixed to the thickness of stiff whipped cream. After covering the tin, I stroked the sides with the back of a fork to obtain a ridged effect and in about two hours, when it was dry, I painted it black and rubbed the surface with bronzing powder which gave it a metallic finish. This shallow dish was greatly admired, and many people asked me where I had bought it.

Another idea is to buy a piece of wood from the local carpenter about 18 inches by 12 inches. And about 2 inches in from all corners, fix cotton reels to act as feet. Then, to one side, or on the centre of this little table, screw an empty tin, either a baking tin or a pie dish. Finally, to ensure that the whole is watertight, insert a second tin inside the first one, and then paint it all black, or any colour you fancy. If you first coat all tins with vinegar and allow them to dry, the paint will adhere much more readily.

When you are painting tins, try flat black mixed with aluminium paint for an antique effect, or mix your paint with sawdust to leave a rough finish, which can finally be brushed over lightly with another colour, the tips of the sawdust just picking up this final coat. Polythene containers can be treated in the same way. I have a number of polythene bleach containers painted black over dull brown sawdust-mixed paint, and my students love them. Incidentally, I fill the bottom of these light polythene containers with stone or gravel to stop them from toppling over.

Bottles and decanters can be made to look elegant or informal, whichever way you wish. I once used a clear-glass wine bottle which I filled with water and added a few spots of red ink. This gave a wonderful, pink, sparkling effect. I then fixed a bowl to the top of the bottle and filled it with pale flowers and variegated ivy - a most effective and cheap container.

You can, if you wish, make an alternative to a Universal bowl, by screwing a pie tin to a cork. To make it watertight, I have often dropped hot sealing-wax over the nail or screw, and in all cases I have painted the tin inside and outside. The cork can then be inserted in a number of bottles and narrow-necked containers.

Another idea you might like to try is that of using an oil funnel for a narrow-necked vase or bottle. One of these can be obtained in plastic or tin at any household store, and after filling in the bottom of the tube to make it watertight, it can be inserted in a bottle, the wide opening at the top being used for the flowers, some trailing downwards.

Wooden workboxes and baskets make most effective containers for garden flowers, but you must always make sure to add a tin or a dish inside to hold the water. When using a basket with a hinged lid, it is often more interesting to make a one-sided arrangement, leaving part of the lid visible. This adds texture and colour-interest to the whole, for if you completely fill a basket, hiding the lid, you may just as well have used a low, round bowl. Similarly, when using a basket with a handle, try to leave part of the handle showing. A handled basket is meant to be functional, to be presented or carried, so do try to make your arrangement so that this is possible.

Containers for pedestals which are used for arrangements at weddings, large halls and at shows are often nothing more than a large tin or a bowl placed on top of the pedestal. When

On top of this Rowhurst forge pedestal is an ordinary bowl filled with crumpled wire netting. It holds pale-green, cream and lemon garden material suitable for a wedding group

working with one of these, I advise you to tie or wire the bowl to the pedestal, otherwise it might tip over. More satisfactory are the new wrought-iron pedestal containers which are now obtainable. These consist of a bowl forged on to an elegant stand, which sometimes extends to adapt to various heights.

Shells can also add texture and colour to an arrangement of leaves. Nearly all shells of reasonable size can be used as containers after being made watertight inside with several coats of varnish or candle wax.

Left half-exposed, the opening holding tiny sedums or a small succulent, the shape of the shell gives a good outline to many decorations. But it is not always as containers that I visualise the beauty of shells. Standing empty at the base of branches, leaves or plants, with the mysterious interior exposed, they can be fascinating points of interest.

Fortunately the treasures we possess in our homes gather more interest with time, but the feeling of change is forever with us. No matter how much is written about containers, the search will always continue for something new.

THE JAPANESE WAY

No book on flower arrangement is complete without some reference to the Japanese art, for it is almost certain that anyone who enjoys arranging will become interested in the Japanese style. At first the appeal may be design, or the philosophy which lies behind the art might be the attraction, but even if the initial appeal is not sustained, I trust the following will satisfy some of the curiosity.

I have always found it fascinating. Its very simplicity, its restraint, its clear-cut lines and the restfulness of the basic designs are enough to hold me in its grip for ever. However, to try to write on Japanese flower arranging in the space of one short heading is rather like

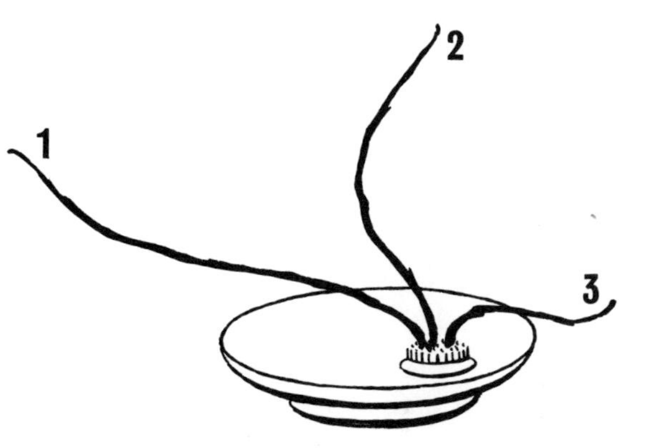

The basic slanting outline used both in Moribana and Nagiere designs. The pin-holder may be placed front, or back, left or right of the shallow dish. The first stem should appear at least one-and-a-half-times the width of the container; the second and third stems should be proportionately two-thirds and one-third the length of the first stem

Moribana basic upright design. The stems are positioned similarly when doing a Nagiere design

Nagiere basic upright

Holders for the upright container, Nagiere style

Crossbar

Forked Kubari

Stem bent to rest on inside of vase

trying to explain the English style in a paragraph or two. It just cannot be done.

There are thousands of schools in Japan, many of them branches of the main ones, and as these schools teach many different designs and there are a great many permutations of each design, you can imagine what space I would need to cover everything, even if I knew it all.

Three of the main schools are known as *Ikenobo ryu* (*ryu* meaning school), *Ohara ryu* and *Sogetsu ryu,* and together these have millions of followers who are always attached to the main source through their teachers, who can prepare students for certificates of proficiency, or for teaching. Proficiency is hardly the word, for the physical movements or technique needed to get the flowers in the vase is not too difficult, especially for those who are already versed in the art of flower arrangement in, say, England or the U.S.A. Instead, it is the philosophy and symbolism that takes the time to learn. This might explain why many discerning people will go to a small school, whose teacher has a reputation of being a fine philosopher, or a creator of character, rather than a large school whose top master they would seldom see, for it is only by learning the philosophy behind the flower arrangement that one learns the lessons of life.

There are ten virtues that are ascribed to those who teach or decide to learn the art. They are:

the prerogative of keeping company with superiors,
ease of manner and worthiness before men of high position,
a calm disposition,
diversion in solitude,
close acquaintance with the nature of plants and trees,
the esteem of mankind,
invariable mildness of character,
wholesomeness of mind and body,
a godly spirit,
self-denial and constraint in feelings.

I recall one occasion when I was taking lessons in Tokyo, when I had a glimpse of the importance of philosophy in Japanese flower arranging. The student next to me was having difficulty in getting her branch to stand on the pin-holder. Each time as she hastily pressed it on a bit harder, the more it seemed to topple, until she almost gave up trying. The teacher came along and took her hand and they both sat on the floor, where he began to talk with her. This lasted for more than half-an-hour, when finally the student picked up the branch again and inserted it on the pin-holder quite calmly and easily. They both then smiled and bowed to each other, she bowing much lower than the teacher, as is the tradition in Japan when a younger person greets or thanks an older person.

Through an interpreter I asked what the teacher had said to her. It was explained to me that he had told her a story of someone who was always struggling against opposition. He had suggested that if she did not struggle *against* the tide, but tried to go *with* it, life would flow more easily, in the manner it was meant to flow. The moral of the story was patience; and so the student was not told an easy, technical way of achieving her end, but by removing force and gently holding the branch, and practising patience, she was shown that the branch could easily be inserted just where she wanted it to go.

There are many symbols and subtle meanings attached to the true art in Japan. For instance, there is the dew-catching leaf which should be placed upward in front, and

This asymmetrical arrangement of flowers from the garden shows deep pink heuchera used for outline with shrub roses and ceanothus in the centre

the dew-dropping leaf which is placed downward at the back. Years ago the students would spend hours learning how to stroke and twist the leaves so that the front and the back were alternately displayed. Sex is also applied to flowers and plants, the front of a leaf is masculine and the underside feminine. Buds are feminine, full flowers are male, yet overblown blossoms are again classed as female. Sex is even applied to the direction of the branches in a classical composition. But flower arranging is a way of life in Japan, and so these regulations are absorbed into the mind from childhood (or at least they used to be) and many are put into practice without thinking.

To complicate things a little more, flowers also have ranks, the chrysanthemum ranking very high. In addition, colours of one variety hold different ranks, white being regarded as a high rank.

The style termed *Shoka* - a more modern version of the old *Rikka* - is that which is most popular with the *Ikenobo* school, and it can be recognised by the manner in which all the stems rise as though bound together for a height of three-and-a-half to four inches above the water level. The stems or branches must be trimmed and made smooth so that they can be placed close together. This strong union of all the stems suggests the trunk of a growing tree.

At the *Ohara* and the *Sogetsu* schools, both now of world renown, the two designs that are taught the most are the *Moribana* style, which is made in a shallow dish, and the *Nagiere* style, which is made in an upright vase. The basic designs of both demand the positioning of three main stems, i.e. heaven, man and earth, to which extra flowers are added low down. The height of the first stem (heaven) should be at least one-and-a-half-times the *width* of the shallow container (Moribana style) or, if making a Nagiere style arrangement, it should be one-and-a-half-times the *height* of the upright container. The second stem should be two-thirds the length of the first, and the third stem should be two-thirds that of the second. These three stems can be placed in a number of ways to represent an upright arrangement, a slanting one or a cascading one.

To understand this a little better, try comparing it with making an English arrangement, when you make the outline first, whether you make an upright, a slanting or a curved arrangement for a mantelshelf, table or hall.

The diagrams on page 53 will explain some of the basic designs, and it may help to know that you could make a Nagiere style arrangement, or a Moribana arrangement, i.e. upright or shallow, following the Ikenobo school, the Sogetsu school or the Ohara school method, or any of the other schools' ways of teaching, for every school will teach the same styles with very slight variations. Different cookery schools will show you varying methods of preparing the same dish, but the end-product will be the same.

Japan is a country of paradoxes, as any Westerner who has travelled there will agree. For instance, some schools refer to the three main lines as *Shin, Soe* and *Tai;* other call them *Shin, So* and *Gio,* while another school refers to them differently again as *Shin, Soe* and *Hikae.* In classical arrangements they are referred to as *Shin, Nagashi* and *Uke,* but in each case they are meant to represent the first, second and third lines of heaven, man and earth, or, to give a deeper meaning, spiritual truth, harmoniser and material substance.

This classical Rikka style arrangement was seen on show in Japan. Rikka is the early-style mass arrangement which was in vogue before Moribana and Nagiere styles became fashionable

Bleached broom was interwoven with branches of oak leaves in a brown pottery container which also held three pink roses. Arrangement by Houn Ohara

Lichen-covered branches and fern made the framework for these orange lilies in a celadine-green container. Arrangement by Houn Ohara

A large pin-holder is used for Moribana arrangements in a shallow dish (remember?), but a *kubari* is used to hold the flowers in place for a Nagiere style in an upright container. A kubari is made from a forked piece of twig which is cut so that it fits snugly into the top of the container. A cross bar is also useful.

A *Morimona* arrangement is one made with fruit, vegetables or flowers, and appears very beautiful when executed by an arranger with sensitivity. The fruit is never piled up, but is allowed to sprawl around on the flat base as though in a still life. Space and restraint are again very important.

As I have already said, there are a great many further styles we could consider but for the serious student there are many good and authoritative books on the market today which can extend her knowledge. I was almost brought up on that intriguing book of Joseph Conder's, *Theory of Japanese Flower Arrangements,* given me by an aunt, but as

The simplicity of this Morimona fruit and flower arrangement is very appealing. Equally attractive from all sides, I made it for a low table

this book is composed of a reprint of a paper read by Mr Conder to the Asiatic Society of Japan in 1889, I am sure much of it must seem old-fashioned now!

However, today as one advances from the basic styles, the student is allowed to give expression in the *Modern Free Style,* where is seems that almost anything can be done. The student can forget all she has previously learnt and can just use her imagination, even if she wants to place branches upside down. This method of Free Style, derived from the West, seems quite out of tune with the Japanese style we thought we knew, even with its complex symbolism.

As with almost everyone today, some Japanese flower arrangers seem to be advancing rather quickly. Not satisfied with their age-old tradition, even with a few up-to-date additions, they have rushed from Free Style to *Avant-garde,* to *Abstract.* Abstract arrangements are also known as non-realistic and need not relate to anything that grows, but in the Avant-garde styled arrangements no flowers are used at all. So when travelling to Japan, as I did, to steep myself in the spiritual calm of the three graceful lines, I saw at many large flower arrangement exhibitions groupings of metal tubing and twisted wires, upturned tree roots, bicycle wheels through which rosettes made of old nylon stockings were protruding. Weird shapes of wood and jagged rocks were grouped in fantastic set pieces, but seldom did I see those three tall graceful lines with flowers added lower down. A lot of these abstract arrangements seemed reminiscent of the crushed car fenders, brilliantly painted, which were exhibited as modern sculpture in New York some time ago, all of which made me want to say to the Japanese flower arrangers - many of whom are my friends - to thine own self be true.

However, since this chapter is meant to enlighten in some small measure, I would add that many of the simple basic designs are most suitable for our modern homes, but they do need space to be seen to advantage.

In conclusion, and for those who are not quite sure how to recognise a Japanese flower arrangement they might see in a flower show these days, I have listed the following points, but I have excluded Free Style, Abstract and Avant-garde from this list:

Flowers should look at each other.

Arrangements should be three-dimensional and not flat. Flowers should not hang downwards. (Paradoxically, in Free Style they may).

They should stretch forward and upward as though reaching for the sun, which may be represented by you.

Try to use odd numbers of flowers. This avoids a regimentated look. Of course, experienced arrangers *can* use even numbers, in fact, many use only two flowers: the one-and-one style which is the arrangement of omission.

Remember that although it is good for a beginner to start with the rules, the rules, just as in English flower arrangements, are there to be broken when you know how.

Problems are often found with presentation flowers on reaching home. Here a triangular pattern is made with the tall stocks on the outside and with the pink roses placed down the centre. Lilies-of-the-valley and freesias flowed forward low down, and the leaves were tucked in the wire around the centre

SEASONAL ARRANGEMENTS

Each season is loved for its own special blooms. Daffodils, tulips, flowering shrubs, paeonies, roses, delphiniums, gladioli, dahlias and chrysanthemums, all follow each other in the garden. The florists' and flower stalls are continuously ablaze with the colour of flowers, so there is nothing to stop us from bringing some of this beauty into the house. Here is some encouragement and help for those who enjoy arranging certain types of seasonal flowers on their own.

TULIPS

A keen flower arranger who uses tulips need never be without inspiration, for there are so many varieties, colours and shapes among these lovely blooms. Whether you use just two blooms as colour interest at the base of a branch for a modern setting, or employ a dozen or more for maximum impact in a mass design, they will always draw attention.

A flowing table-centre made in a silver entrée dish, with lovely lily-flowering tulips such as the China Pink variety, combined with grey foliage of centaurea, is very satisfactory. No matter how these lily-flowering tulips twist and turn, they are always fascinating, and as the flowers open more widely the interest becomes even greater.

My favourites early in the year are the double tulips, for they are shorter of stem and open up so well that you seem to need fewer of them to make a display. As I write, I have three pure-white double tulips, spaced well at the base of a tall spray of andromeda with its panicles of white lily-of-the-valley-like flowers drooping down at the top.

The paeony-flowered tulips are best for large groups as they are a good central item when combined with early, leafy twigs or branches of stripped lime. I have used sulphur-yellow paeony-flowered tulips with pale-green lime twigs to great effect, but the rose-pink Eros variety also looks very lovely with pale-green lime.

I must admit, with tulips, I love additional

A roll of plastic-covered garden fencing was here stood over a well pin-holder which held water. A tall swerving branch of corylopsis was inserted on to the holder, the design being finished with two short stems of orange-coloured clivias. Two clivia leaves finished the effect

foliage such as mahonia or laurustinus, so I do advise new garden owners to plant a few evergreen shrubs. The sight of a leaf or two in winter and early spring is always welcome in the garden and useful for decoration. You can form an interesting group by adding some of the spurges with tulips. I once picked wild caper spurge from some open ground and placed the stem ends in hot water for a few seconds, then in deep cool water, to make it turgid and appear more straight and strong. Everyone asked what the beautiful lime-green flower was!

The striped Rembrandt tulips are also fast becoming favourites for decoration because of their candy-striped effect. I love the variety called Calypso, which has broad stripes and streaks of white on a cerise background. I have used a few of these in an old pewter lamp-stand with a pie tin fixed in the top. I find that tulips cut short last much longer than if the stems are left long, and they also stay in place better.

A copper kettle is another good container for tulips with blossom. Backed by a tray, this combination looks ideal placed on a table or an oak chest in the hall. Fill the kettle with crumpled wire netting and place curved sprays of blossom or leafy twigs to form a crescent-shaped outline, then mass the tulips in the centre. Try white blossom and yellow tulips in brass, or pink blossom with crimson tulips in copper.

Tulips and flowering shrubs grace our garden at the same time. So if we can afford to pick a few tulips, or even a single spray of a flowering shrub, we are sure to be able to watch living beauty unfold in the home before our eyes.

Last year at spring-time, I remember making a design with white blossom, pale lemon-coloured tulips and the pale green-flowered *Helleborus corsicus*. Around the centre I placed those fascinating leaves of *Arum italicum marmoratum,* which have a green-and-white marbled appearance. These leaves grow wild in many parts of the country, but a number of flower arrangers are now cultivating them, for they are so effective in spring designs.

Tulips last well; in fact I find that I like them better at the end of a week, when their petals are wide open revealing the stamens, than I do when they are tightly closed.

Apple-green foliage is a pleasant combination with tulips of any colour, so look for leaves that have been starved of light to get that pale yellowish-green hue. I often cut green curly kale leaves, then stand them in water in the dark for a few days, when the leaves will turn a yellowish-green. If you add a teaspoonful of salt to the water, it helps remove the odour of cut kale leaves.

Extra foliage is not always available, so do treat tulip leaves with care, for if they are submerged in water overnight to make them turgid, they will add considerably to your decoration.

It is not always possible to pick enough tulips to make a big display, but I find that tulips bought from the florists' last a long time, especially if the stems are re-cut, placed in deep water to which a teaspoonful of sugar has been added, and left in this for some hours before arranging.

DAFFODILS

As the stems of daffodils are bare and straight they are not the easiest flowers to arrange, and the leaves, although providing a soft touch of green, are not broad enough to add depth to any design.

Pale-pink tulips were placed down the centre of this design featuring cherry blossom, Helleborus orientalis *and primulas*

To appear effective in the home, daffodils need the accompaniment of other plant material - pussy willow or alder catkins, forsythia or any twisted branches - together with some broader leaves such as mahonia, small rhododendron, kale or skimmia.

Try using the gay blooms of daffodils standing upright in a brown jug or basketware tray, adding wild arum leaves low down, together with some moss. You could also combine them with mimosa, treating this by re-cutting the stem ends and leaving them in hot water for an hour before using. Another appealing combination is to arrange purple anemones with yellow daffodils, as these colours are perfect complementaries.

Daffodils look more attractive if the stems are cut to different lengths so that no two heads stand level with each other. If you allow some to turn sideways and some backwards even, the finished effect is more natural than if all the flowers are facing forwards. Daffodils will also last longer if the ends of the stems are squeezed under warm water to wash away the slimy substance that is exuded.

Florists now sell bunches of daffodils that include buds, so if you do not want to pick blooms from your garden you can create a natural design with a few bought from the florist, adding foliage gathered from the garden or countryside.

Daffodils do not lend themselves to 'swerving' formal designs. Just the same, there

(Left) Three tulips are placed in the neck of a green wine bottle at the base of a few stems of pussy willow

(Right) Five lemon-coloured tulips placed at the base of a tall lichen-covered branch formed this simple design for a modern home. A shorter branch tilted out at the left with an even shorter one low at the right. Mahonia leaves gave depth round the centre

(Left) Pussy willow and pale-green leaf sprays of hawthorn give height to the daffodils in this Easter design which is given a final touch by the placement of two china 'bunnies'

(Above) This unusual arrangement of daffodils placed in a tea pot claims originality because of the placement of the twisted wood spreading out to the left

is nothing more refreshing than daffodils placed upright, down through the centre of the arrangement, while other flowers such as tulips or freesias, and swerving twigs, are placed at the sides and forward in front. *Viburnum opulus* (snowball tree) makes an ideal addition to such a design, for it is pale green in the spring and its round flower head can be tucked in near the wire to hide any bareness.

As daffodils usually look their best when arranged naturally, I never really enjoy seeing them falling down at the sides of a design. However, not all settings call for the natural expression. For instance, at a big banquet, you could not imagine them on the table, arranged with pieces of wood, fungus and moss. Here they would fit in best grouped with shorter bright-red tulips and perhaps orange clivia and green viburnum. The compact colours of these would have to compete with the splendour of their setting.

So when you see a design you do not like, try not to decry it at once. Attempt to find out the intention behind it. This constructive appraisal will awaken your critical instincts and help you to avoid falling into a rut with your own designs.

ANEMONES

In the spring, there is nothing more gay than the brightly coloured anemones which are so plentiful. Millions of bunches of them will be sold throughout late winter and early spring, and few of us can resist these flowers which are so colourful at this time of year - even if they do sometimes appear in the florists' shops as colourless, plastic-like balls with a green fringe collar on the end of a stem!

If you cut and pinch the stem ends and place them in a jug of warm water, to which half-a-teaspoonful of sugar has been added, these blooms will open wide in the warmth of a room, displaying their vividly coloured petals, with mysterious black anthers at their centres. They also last well, closing and opening as the warmth of the room dictates.

A bowl of these flowers placed under a lamp on a small table will add gaiety to any room, and when combined with various 'bits' from the garden, such as laurustinus, ivy, veronica, even aucuba, they make a very cheerful table decoration.

I once arranged some anemones with forsythia and skimmia in a shallow basket. As the basket was not watertight, I used a fine-pinned Wonder pin-holder in a tin of water, which was stood inside the basket. Skimmia, by the way, is an evergreen shrub I would not be without, for apart from the attractive rosettes of leaves, its small flowers are effective at this time of year, and later the bright red berries surpass those of the holly in brilliance.

IRISES

Our Anglo-Saxon ancestors grew the common *Iris germanica* in their monastery gardens, and many country cottage gardens are still ablaze with their royal-purple petals every year in May, adding a special charm to the late spring scene.

Yet these are by no means the only irises used in home decoration, as so many new hybrids have been introduced of recent years.

Spanish irises are with us for quite a long time in the year, for not only can they be grown in the garden, but they are also a market-grown flower obtainable in the florists' shops.

Most of us recognise the common yellow flag iris, *Iris pseudacorus,* when we see it

Six pale-blue iris here complemented the line of the salted grey drift-wood placed on a black base – a muted arrangement which was finished with sprigs of Choisya ternata, *an evergreen shrub*

growing by the sides of lakes and pools. I have found it long lasting and very effective in arrangements, its pale lemon colouring associating well with light-green hosta leaves.

The petals of the bearded iris appear rather fragile, but as a number of flowers are found on each stem, you can often remove the lower one as it fades, making way for the bud above it to open.

If used in simple or restrained designs, irises give a stately appearance, but for inclusion in a mass arrangement they are better grouped in the centre as main interest, for they look unhappy when placed at the sides in an almost prone position.

A good way to create a decorative effect with irises is by just placing them (cut to different lengths) one below the other on a pin-holder in a shallow dish surrounded low down with leaves. The double *Iris kaempferi,* however, need more careful handling, for these beautiful flat-topped irises are too lovely to be cut down. They need to stand upright in all their glory.

Some of us can go out and pick additional foliage, and the inclusion of some leaves low down in a design with irises usually makes it much more effective. However, stones or pieces of wood can be substituted instead. A few irises, stood on a pin-holder rising from a shallow dish filled with water, will make a very attractive picture, giving the tranquil effect of a pool.

DELPHINIUMS

It is true that the British are recognised all over the world for the beauty of their herbaceous borders, and over these the delphinium reigns supreme. Lately, growers have been giving us shorter-stemmed varieties, which are a pleasure to all those who love to cut them for decoration.

Admittedly we usually think of delphiniums as blue, but today there is a lovely range of colours from which the flower arranger may choose.

It is difficult to imagine a summer wedding without delphiniums in tall pedestal vases at the reception, or as large groups each side of the chancel steps in the church.

These lovely spikes are ideal for the outline of large arrangements, forming a background for larger or rounder flowers, such as paeonies, lilies and hydrangeas. The lateral stems of delphiniums are ideal for smaller formal arrangements, suitable for any medium-sized sitting-room. Some of you may like to follow my idea of pinching off the main spike quite early in growth, which allows the laterals to form in greater abundance and strength. The side stems of these are more pliant and not hollow, and will give the soft curves which are so suitable for side placements in a vase. While discussing side laterals, I must remind you how well these dry for winter decorations. Pick them before they are fully in flower and hang them in small bunches upside down in a dark, dry cupboard. The darkness will help retain their colour.

Single florets, picked off the main stem, are also ideal for smaller arrangements and one of the most interesting table decorations I have made was of lemons placed over chicken wire through which blue delphinium flowers were inserted. The pink or crushed-strawberry colour of Astolat seedlings have much appeal, especially when arranged with grey onopordum thistle leaves. I like the lighter yellow-green hosta leaves with the

An early hazel catkin branch gives height to this naturalistic arrangement of daffodils on a wooden base. Blue muscari in phials of water were stood between the moss and wood which covered the well pin-holder

deeper or greeny-blue delphiniums, although all grey leaves seem to combine well with the various shades of these flowers.

Delphiniums last well if they are picked when not too open. Cut late at night, then re-cut under water in a pail. Given a long drink before arranging, they will stand up well. Ronald Parrett's steel-grey Toledo is charming for arrangers.

PAEONIES

I am often asked the name of my favourite flower, and always find it difficult to answer. So much depends upon the season and the reason for its use. However, so far as my favourite flower *and* leaf, are concerned, I have no hesitation in naming the paeony, in all its variations.

Consider its stem for decorative work. It is wonderfully strong and is not always dead straight, unless it is staked in that manner. Picked in bud, the beautiful blooms will go on unfolding for a long time, and when fully opened they are a delight, looking like crushed silk.

The leaves are a tremendous asset to a flower arranger. In fact, long after the bloom has died in the garden, the leaves continue in their reddish, dark green and bronzy stages, to give us useful foliage well on into autumn. And paeonies, whether used alone or with taller flowers such as delphiniums, will always give an attractive display.

For the table, I once used three pink paeonies in a low dish tucked between grey stones picked up from Brighton beach. They were beautifully veined with mauve and white, and could not have looked better had they been expensive carved marble.

Tall twigs and branches are another good item to associate with these large, round flowers. Keep your eyes open for interesting pieces of wood and stones, and try them in different ways with your paeonies. There is no one to say you cannot put this with that. You are the artist, so at home do as you like. In show work, of course, you abide by the schedule.

Five single white paeonies standing one below the other on a pin-holder in a large Swedish glass dish make a simple effective arrangement. The bud goes at the top and the larger flowers low down, surrounded by leaves. Glass marbles in the base of the dish could cover the pin-holder and give a little extra decorative effect.

If you grow a number of varieties, nothing is more lovely than to have a mass of paeonies in the house. By grouping white, pale pink, cream and crimson flowers you can have a picture which will delight family and friends alike.

SWEET PEAS

Sweet peas, with their delicacy and delightful perfume, are a delight to use as cut flowers in the home. Most growers will supply you with cultural hints, and the National Sweet Pea Society is a mine of information. Here are a few additional suggestions of varieties to grow for the most interesting schemes, and plant material to use with sweet peas.

The types to aim for are those with the most interesting colours, to combine with other foliage, and I find them best grown up a string trellis, for this gives swerves and twisted stems, and allows for a number of grey tendrils to be picked. A most exciting sweet pea is Unwin's Fantasy, a cream flower, veined and picotee-edged with chocolate; arranged with grey leaves and with an additional touch of lemon it is most arresting.

Lichen-covered twigs and catkins were placed at the back of these cerise-coloured anemones in a Denby-ware tea pot. Laurustinus filled in the design

Many of the striped varieties are quite unusual and appealing in decorative schemes, while bi-colours give that 'extra something' so necessary for prize winning.

A scheme featuring mauve and purple sweet peas, with perhaps the carmine-rose Jupiter, combined with grey *Artemisia ludoviciana* or grey centaurea, or even reddish-purple strawberry leaves picked from low on the plant, would make an appealing picture. Elizabeth Taylor is a lovely clear, deep mauve, rich in colouring and with a most pleasing satiny softness.

Of course, sweet peas give a perfect finish to the sides and front of mixed schemes, and can be used advantageously in any spot where flowing swerves are needed. The flowers are easily held in place by crumpled wire-netting, and if you want to be quite sure of their firmness, try wiring two or three stems together and inserting them as wired on to a pin-holder.

Although we so often associate sweet peas with dainty glass, silver or china, try putting them with contrasting items which are more straight or solid.

Small hosta leaves are good for uniting the stems towards the bottom, while swordlike montbretia leaves make a good soaring background. Pale-green dock or sorrel, sprays of berberis and ivy are all good additions.

In all cases sweet peas should be placed loosely with plenty of space between the stems.

If the weather is hot, do not make the mistake of spraying sweet peas with water, as this will leave blotches on the petals.

GLADIOLI

Almost every flower arranger tries her hand at arranging gladioli sooner or later, yet many say they find them difficult. Personally, I find them easy. True, their stems are stiff and straight and they are sometimes considered ungraceful, but they are dramatic in form. If you want grace, then you must add some flowing leaves or branches. Gladioli are long-lasting when cut, and as the lower flowers die so others open higher up the stem, until you can work with only the twisted tips to make interesting designs incorporating drift-wood or foliage.

The bigger varieties are excellent for a strong, central line in pedestal groups for large halls and churches. For home decoration, many arrangers are inclining towards the primulinus and butterfly types of gladioli which are smaller and easier to handle.

One of my most satisfying gladioli schemes was composed of Unwin's primulinus Sulphur Gem. This is a sulphur-greenish colour, and with it I placed pale-green Jacob's ladder (the wild reseda) for additional spikes, and unripe green grapes low down, together with some kale leaves that I had kept indoors in the dark to lighten their colour. These were placed on a black base which dramatised the pale-green colourings above it.

Ice Follies is the name of a ruffled, white butterfly gladiolus which looks most effective, and some of the pink varieties such as Bo-Peep and Crinklette are also well worth trying. They lend a delicate air to a formal room setting, especially when combined with grey foliage, *Begonia rex* and some of the smaller kale leaves. When using kale for decoration submerge it overnight in water to which some salt has been added. The salt will remove the odour of kale. The butterfly varieties, Mecky and Daily Sketch, are a further two that are ideal for the fashionable peachy-beige colourings. Combined with lime-green euphorbia

White delphiniums are here combined with pink, single rambler roses in a Meisen china container. Ash leaves drew the stems together

(Above) This off-centre arrangement of white delphiniums was completed with yellow roses in the centre, backed with hosta leaves

(Right) This beautiful Chinese single paeony from Waterer is called White Wings and is here seen arranged in a grey-green container with philadelphus

Pink and crimson paeonies are here grouped in a Victorian mahogany tea chest. A dish was filled with crumpled wire netting and stood inside the box

Here the same tea chest is filled with white philadelphus and pink sweet peas. Small roses add depth around the centre

(Above) Pink gladioli and pink dahlias are here grouped on a pin-holder behind a large piece of root wood to make this modern design

(Right) This upright arrangement of gladioli was made on a brass trivet. Stood in a well pin-holder, the flowers were united at the left with large bergenia leaves with Sedum spectabile *at the right*

(Far right) This huge bowl of pink and cream roses made a beautiful sight placed in this home setting

(Above) These exquisite Royal Worcester salt cellars, only three inches in width, held miniature roses. Varieties Pour Toi at top and Pixie bottom right

(Right) In a glass container these white spider chrysanthemums were grouped with pale green Cobaea scandens *and white symphoricarpos berries, all held in wet Oasis*

(common spurge) and green hart's-tongue ferns, they make a striking effect. When using bold red gladioli in a modern design I like to add the large green leaves of *Fatsia japonica* or hosta, often adding a piece of drift-wood low down.

The large gladioli require a heavy pin-holder to hold them firmly in place, but they make a bold effect, especially at a party. Of course, all gladioli associate well with other flowers, but I prefer to use them for the height and centre of a design and I would advise you not to stick them low down from each side of a classic vase, like stiff arms.

Remember when picking or buying these flowers to re-cut them under water and leave them for a long, deep drink before finally placing them. Look for strong forms to associate with gladioli, and you will be pleased with the result.

ROSES

No flower offers more interesting material to the floral artist than the rose. It has so many variations in texture, form, colour and size that the perfect rose can be found for every occasion.

After picking or buying roses, re-cut the stem ends under water and remove the lower leaves, allowing the stems to remain in deep water for some hours before arranging them. Cutting the stem ends under water avoids an air-lock and allows more water to rise into the flower head.

To make an interesting design you will require roses of different lengths. After making the stalks shorter, split the ends before inserting them into the vase. Have water already in the vase to prevent the stems from becoming dry, and add Chrysal, Gregory's Rose Preservative or Bio flowerlife to the water to help make the blooms last longer.

I prefer to see roses used only with their own foliage, but often, when requiring a large design or when using roses bought from the florist, additional foliage is a help.

I am inclined to agree with the many people who ask if it is really necessary to *arrange* roses, for I must admit that they are very beautiful in themselves. Yet, despite their natural beauty, it is helpful to know how to place them in a vase to greater effect. If thoughtlessly stood in a container they will remain a mass of specimen stems, but if these same roses are cut to different lengths and inserted in some crumpled wire netting, reserving the biggest blooms for the centre, a much more decorative effect will be achieved.

You do not, however, need a lot of roses to make a decoration, for a single bloom placed in a wine bottle backed by a twisted vine spray will make a picture, while a few light-vermilion Super Star roses grouped on a pin-holder at the base of a tall green twig will make a very eye-catching design.

Many people love to grow roses not only for the beauty they give in the garden but also for their attractiveness in the home. Others love them for their perfume, and although not all modern roses are scented, here is my choice of a few which are: Madame Louis Laperrière, Crimson Glory, the Doctor, Geranium Red, Red Ensign and Fragrant Cloud, and the new pink hybrid tea rose Lady Seton (named after me, in my married name) which won the Clay Cup in 1964 at the National Rose Society for the most highly perfumed rose of the year grown by a British grower.

Considering the number of new roses that the breeders and growers introduce each year, we certainly ought to have a fine selection of

Two stems of single spray chrysanthemums were here used as main interest below the bulrushes in this green basket arrangement. Canary grass was used diagonally and brown wild dock was placed at the left. A well pin-holder was used

varieties to choose from when it comes to home decoration. In fact, however, many small modern gardens have room for only a few bushes, and my correspondence proves that a great many flower arrangers are deterred from cutting freely for the house for fear of spoiling the appearance of the garden.

Even if you pick only one truss from a bush of floribundas, you can make an attractive decoration. And what lovely floribundas there are available! I love John Church, which is an orange-red with hybrid tea type blooms, and repeats its flowering all summer. Or if you want a feminine-looking rose, you could not do better than grow the peach-pink floribunda Violet Carson. I enjoy arranging Sale's browny-tan varieties Café and Fantan, especially with any lime-green coloured additions. Le Grice's Lavender Pinocchio is a very unusual lavender blue-grey colour.

Another good idea for using a few roses is to place each short stem in a tube of water and insert these between fruit for a table decoration, or between leaves in a grouping of house plants.

If I were called upon to make a large pedestal or wedding group, I would choose the distinctive peach-coloured rose of Dickson's called Apricot Nectar; or another from Dickson's, Sea Pearl, which is a little more pink. Both have the long stems that give graceful swerves.

CHRYSANTHEMUMS

It is often difficult to know what to put with chrysanthemums, for although they are long-lasting the leaves are rather uninteresting from a flower arranger's point of view. If you are clever, you can use the 'all-round' chrysanthemums on their own by recessing some here and there, but usually these blooms require some broad leaves to create depth for the design, or some fine-pointed items to form a framework.

With yellow and bronze chrysanthemums, try the broad leathery bergenia (megasea) leaves. If you completely submerge these leaves in water overnight before using them, they will last for weeks. Green laurel, rhododendron, hosta and kale leaves are all excellent foils, and for outline interest you could try wild dock, Jacob's ladder, astilbes or *Atriplex hortensis rosea,* commonly called mountain spinach. This last is most effective with the pink - and maroon-coloured chrysanthemums, for it is a dark maroon shade, and although it grows from seed to a height of four feet or more, the side sprays give soft swerves. An outline of atriplex with pink spray chrysanthemums, interspersed with grey centaurea foliage and perhaps black privet berries, is a lovely combination.

I find most ornamental grasses too fine to place with chrysanthemums, but feathery carrot and beetroot leaves are ideal for certain colour schemes.

You do not need a lot of chrysanthemums to make an interesting design. Recently I placed a green wine bottle on a tray and behind it a dish with a pin-holder and water in which I inserted some tall sprays of greenish-brown dock and then three chrysanthemums grouped behind and in front of the bottle. The dish was hidden with kale leaves, and the finished design looked most effective on the sideboard.

All chrysanthemum stems, being semi-woody, need to be broken or split just before using to allow better intake of water, which should be already in the vase before you begin arranging the blooms to avoid the stems drying.

The short stems of blooms from two long stems of spray chrysanthemums were here placed at the base of dry manzanita wood. A few skeletonised magnolia leaves gave extra effect to this design in a shallow bowl on a black wooden base

(Above) A few yellow chrysanthemums are here grouped in a tin bowl fixed to an old swinging lamp-stand. Bulrushes and wild dock give height

(Right) Royal-blue anchusa and lavender-blue iris made this simple design in a crimson glass water jug. No holder was required. A few variegated leaves covered the rim

The beautiful variety called Green Nightingale, from Woolman's of Shirley, Birmingham, is a gem for decoration. Pale-green in colour, its petals are fine and curved at the ends, sometimes being called spoon-like or spider-like. Fine of stem, it assorts with many types of foliage, and if you add white *Symphoricarpus albus* (snowberry tree) and use green-and-white hosta leaves, you can arrive at a most unusual green-and-white scheme.

I am also very fond of the single chrysanthemums, which bloom mainly in November. Woolman has these in yellow, pink, white, crimson and orange. I can guarantee that any arrangement made with the single yellow Peggy Stevens grouped with green foliage will arouse admiration from all who see it. And by combining the pink Preference with green grapes you will produce a dramatic design.

DAHLIAS

Dahlias are among the easiest of flowers to grow, so it is not surprising that they are featured prominently in many of the autumn horticultural shows. In the home they are also great favourites for decoration, since they combine so well with a number of the late border flowers and leaves. And yet many housewives state that they find cut dahlias do not last very long.

I can't agree with this. If the flowers are cut and the stem ends are then stood in about 2 inches of very hot water for a few seconds, they should easily last a week. Naturally, after the hot-water treatment the vase should be filled with warm water, but it is this few seconds' immersion in the hot water which seals the ends and prevents the loss of the white substance exuded from the stems.

The finer-stemmed varieties, particularly the small decoratives and the pompons, last well without this treatment, but I do advise you to make some experiments for yourself.

Solidago, michaelmas daisies and the tall spikes of purple liatris, as well as the maroon-coloured atriplex and kniphofia (red-hot pokers), all make good, spire-like contrasts to the roundness of dahlias, but do make sure to place the dahlias down the centre or in a main part of the arrangement, leaving the more spiky flowers to form the outline.

The small cactus dahlia named Almeh, which is a light fuchsia-purple, makes a delightful decoration when placed with the tall liatris and grey onopordum thistle leaves, and if a few light green grapes are added or any pale green seed heads, the effect is immediately highlighted.

Many flower arrangers prefer the warmer colours to combine with the numerous autumn-tinted leaves, and such cactus varieties as Carnaval and Golden Heart, which are both reddish-orange, look well with the yellow solidago and orange-red kniphofias.

I am rather attracted to the fimbriated type of dahlia, for the fine-fluted petal edges give such a light effect. I once arranged a pink one I particularly like, called Popular Guest, with poppy seed-heads and grey foliage on a polished dinner table, flanked with silver candle-sticks and pink candles. Other unusual types which I am sure will appeal to the flower arranger are the Collerette dahlias - look out for them in florists' shops or when visiting autumn flower shows.

(Page 92) This wrought iron sculpture by Aczel held three pink paeonies to form this modern design

(Page 93) The highly-scented tea rose Lady Seton, arranged in a formal gilded container. Stems held by crumpled wire netting

(Left) These four carnations give a dominant note to this modern grouping of drift-wood and curled broom. Short stems of Helleborus corsicus *were added*

A round bowl of dahlias is ideal for the centre of a table. Here a coral-coloured variety is arranged with stems of pale-green ivy buds

(Left) These lovely pale-pink dahlias are named Gerrie Hoek and are excellent for decoration. All held in wire netting, some variegated foliage and crimson polygonum stems were added

Copper makes ideal containers for the warmer colours of peach and flame, whereas brass is ideal for the lemons and yellows. The lavender and purple colours are ideally suited to pewter, so do give these metals a trial with your favourite dahlias.

CARNATIONS

In winter months the perpetual-flowering carnations really come into their own, and even if you do not grow these lovely greenhouse flowers yourself there are always plenty to be bought in the florists' shops.

Carnations lend themselves to delightful colour schemes. I love the delicate colouring of Allwood's Market Apricot arranged with lime-green ferns or brown, dried beech and other leaves - an eye-catcher in any grouping. Try a few blooms of this colouring arranged in a dish with some leaves and placed on a brown tray. Add a bunch of pale-green grapes lying on the tray and hiding the dish. You will enjoy this effect, placed on a table.

Many people ask me what foliage or other plants can be successfully combined with carnations, and in winter-time I nearly always recommend ferns. But I do find the foliage of carrots and parsley very accommodating and when using pink carnations, such as Monty's Pale Rose, I like a framework of maroon-coloured beetroot leaves or the ornamental-leaved kale. All these leaves need to be submerged in water for many hours before being used, and if a spoonful of sugar is added to the water they will remain turgid and strong for much longer.

Of course a number of florists sell carnation foliage, which is ideal - it is called carnation grass in the trade - and you can also buy grevillea and eucalyptus foliages.

I also like arranging carnations with wood, providing this is not too heavy. Dry brown dock and grasses, even wheat and oats, are all good additions for carnation arrangements, and remember, when flowers are in short supply, that even one fresh carnation arranged in a bottle with a branch, can prove most attractive.

TERRARIUMS

Speaking to a newly formed group of flower and garden enthusiasts during late winter recently, I was asked if I could make a few creative suggestions that would keep the members interested, yet would not involve spending money on expensive spring flowers, since many of them were pensioners with only very small gardens and incomes.

Apart from making landscape designs, the material for which some younger members could collect, I was reminded of the very attractive terrariums (gardens in glass) that I saw recently at a flower show in the USA.

Some very unusual containers had been brought into service. Old coach lamps, dimpled whisky bottles, oil lamp funnels stood over a mound of soil on a base, as well as fish bowls and gas globes, all played their part in this attractive collection.

I always have one of these miniature gardens standing under a lamp during winter and spring, and find it requires very little attention, yet always appears so alive and fascinating that I often sit and gaze at it.

In a goldfish bowl, I planted a small hart's-tongue fern with some wild primroses and a piece of tradescantia at the right. I picked off the primroses as they faded, but the foliage was attractive for many weeks. Sometimes, if I have a few small flowers such as wild cyclamen or violets, I place them in a small bottle of water, and insert the bottle in the

Carnations are everyone's standby. Here in this glass cornucopia-shaped vase are pink carnations and pink single stocks with broom. A little wire netting at the top of the vase held the stems

soil. They appear to be growing and give an extra touch of colour.

Another miniature garden I have is in a brandy glass, and should you wish to make one for yourself, start by putting in an inch of gravel to which some charcoal has been added, covering this with an inch or two of sandy soil. You can have the soil higher one side, if you like, if your terrarium is to be viewed from one angle, and you might like to add a piece of bark, some twisted wood or stones for a scenic effect.

You can cover the soil surface with moss - and there are so many attractive mosses to be found by those who keep their eyes open. Then, with a pencil or spoon, make holes in the soil in which to place your plants. I used a plantlet of chlorophytum and a small piece of tradescantia in the front, adding a small fern (picked off a damp wall) and some snowdrop bulbs at the back, as well as a shell and a tiny model owl for fun. The 'garden' was lightly watered, and I usually keep a lid on the glass to keep in moisture, removing it now and again for ventilation and to avoid condensation on the glass. If after a while a plant appears unhappy, I remove it and replace it with another, which all adds to the interest.

These terrariums would make a good lesson at a club meeting or a new class at a spring show. Why not include them and give all members a chance to try their hands?

POT ET FLEUR

Most of us at times wish that life were more easy. Whenever this feeling creeps over me when in London in winter when flowers are rare or expensive, and friends descend unannounced on me, I lovingly run to my potted plants and add a few living cut flowers for my decorations.

This terrarium in a brandy glass makes an ideal living decoration for the winter

This style of indoor decoration is termed *Pot-et-Fleur* and is exactly what it says - potted plants with flowers added.

I first saw this type of decoration at a show in the USA where it was shown as an answer for those who live in flats or modern houses where gardens are small, but I love them anywhere and at any time, in fact I am seldom without them myself.

To copy the idea, you need to group about three indoor plants together: those that live happily together are the best choice for watering, although I sometimes add a *Begonia rex*, only to remove it when I spray the others with water. (Do remember that *Begonia rex* likes to drink from the bottom and any water spilled on the leaves will only finish in a brown rot.) However, you need not include *Begonia rex* in your assortment, for three easy plants can be chosen among the following: *Cissus antartica* (kangaroo vine), *Philodendron scandens* (sweetheart vine), *Rhoicissus rhomboidea* (grape ivy) or sansevieria (mother-in-law's tongue) for height. The chlorophytum (spider plant) and *Peperomia magnoliaefolia* (desert privet) give variegated change of form and the ivies and tradescantia (wandering Jew) will give trails for flowing over the rim of vase or container. All the plants I have mentioned above are very easy to care for and there are many more, but it is better to start with those which do not disappoint you, then study the needs of others as you wish to widen your range of plants and gain variety of texture and size. Antony Huxley has written a book, *House Plants*, for such as you and I who wish to know the needs of these fascinating plants.

Shown on page 105 is a *pot-et-fleurs* made with a sansevieria plant for height. I left this in its original pot, for I grew it from a cutting and was loth to change its home just yet. At the left low down is a peperomia (desert privet) in pale green and yellow and top right is a plant of canariensis ivy, also green-and-white. Low at right is a new plant of *Zebrina pendula* (silver with mauve stripes) which had just rooted from cuttings and was kept in a plastic bag of wet sand and soil until I found it a permanent home. Then in between the pots I added a slice of wet Oasis (a green plastic substance bought from a florist) and into this I inserted five pink Garnette roses. It was a lovely colour scheme with the roses giving a highlight and when the roses faded, I had the pleasure of knowing it was not much trouble to replace them with five other flowers. The plants did not need to be removed from their container for watering.

Much larger groups can be made using large plants such as tall dracaena (dragon plant) and the large-leaved dieffenbachia (dumb cane) with crotons. These plants however need skilled attention and understanding, although if you buy a Rochford plant these bear labels which are coloured pink for an easy plant to grow, blue for an intermediate, and yellow for a delicate plant.

With the larger groupings you can add just one stem of say *Lilium rubrum,* the red-spotted pink lily. This can be placed in a tube of water which is inserted in the pot. Tubes or small phials of water are ideal for holding flowers to be inserted into plant arrangements, but I nearly always add a piece of Oasis stood in a tin of water, for it is quite easy then to insert the additional flowers.

A small block of wet Oasis was used to hold the six flame coloured carnations which I introduced into a basket design. I love this basket, for it is tin-lined, and potted plants stand happily in it, any surplus water being able to stay in the tin lining. Here I used *Rhoicissus rhomboidea* (grape ivy) used for height, with chlorophytum tilted out low at the left. Over the rim of the basket I planted a variegated ivy, and at the back a browny-grey maroon *Begonia rex.* I loved this grouping for the variation of size and texture of plants, and almost all flowers go well with it, but remember to remove the *Begonia rex* when watering, and water this on its own from the bottom.

You will have endless joy with this type of decoration for the plants are always growing, and the dominant interest can be changed with just a few cut flowers as the mood takes you.

A tall, leafless branch gave effect to this winter arrangement of snowdrops in bottles of water 'planted' in the moss which covered the holder

Four potted plants are here grouped in a lidded basket to which five lemon-coloured carnations are added held in wet Oasis. The Cissus antarctica *gives height, the striped chlorophytum swerved out at the left and a* Begonia rex *can be seen on the right with ivy in between*

The tall sansevieria plant was placed at the back of this container while Hedera canariensis *can be seen at the right together with a* Zebrina pendula *and a peperomia at the left. Five pale-pink roses were inserted into wet Oasis and placed between the pots*

SPECIAL OCCASIONS

Since I wrote my first book, *Fun with Flowers,* great advancement has been made in the world of flower arrangement. It has become a social grace, and many thousands of women have found a new interest and outlet through this expressive art. There is no doubt that flowers are steadily assuming an ever-increasing importance in our lives.

Despite this I find that, as more and more books on entertaining appear, references to flowers at parties are often either relegated to the back of the book, or written off with just one page of description. Is this, I wonder, because flowers are *expected* to be present, and so need no more qualification for inclusion in the book?

This omission has always seemed a pity to me. While agreeing that food and drink are important at parties, I would like to see the floral decorations lifted from the accepted part they so often play and promoted to one of the star roles-even that of prima ballerina!

Pink pinks and white gypsophila are here grouped in wet Oasis held in a candle-cup on the top of a cherub stand, to form the table decoration for a christening party. Dishes of sugared almonds surrounded the arrangement

Some of the most successful parties I have attended or have given have been planned round the flowers. At such events they certainly have been talked about, not only because 'they are lovely' (all flowers are lovely) but because they have played an important interpretive part in the overall party scheme.

This chapter is an extension of my reflections on flower arrangement in connection with parties, written to fill what I think is a gap, giving hints and ideas on how flowers can help you to toe the party line. While not purposely contriving to be different for the sake of it, I always enjoy introducing novelties to surprise and delight my guests, and I hope you will like some of these ideas.

COCKTAIL PARTY ARRANGEMENTS

Flowers should play an important part as decorations at a cocktail party. In fact, if their use is exaggerated, they can assume a star role. In the early part of the year, try using only mimosa as your flower scheme. I have done this with great success, but you must use it profusely, displaying masses of it on the mantelshelf, tables and pedestals, so that it becomes the talk of the gathering and

This table arrangement was made of six white iris and a dozen yellow tulips held by wire netting in a low dish

is remembered. Order a basket (or more) of mimosa direct from your florist, and ask for it to be delivered in the basket. If you recut the stems before placing them in very hot water to swell the wood, and then arrange the sprays in warm water to which a little sugar has been added, you will find they will stay fresh and fluffy for quite a long time.

Not only does the colour of this delightful blossom add gaiety to the winter atmosphere; the skip baskets in which the flowers travel to our flower markets from the south of France can be used as containers for your tit-bits and *canapés.* Fix the lid open with wire, line the basket with greaseproof paper or table napkins on which the food is placed, and for extra effect attach a spray of mimosa to the open lid with perhaps some mauve ribbon.

Sometimes an intimate gathering at home calls for flowers that do not take up too much room. Here is a pyramid of yellow daisies grouped in a vase on a cake-stand in a sugar bowl

To carry the idea a little further, serve a mimosa cocktail. This is really delicious, and if you have not yet tried it you have a pleasure to come. Use one-third Benedictine, one-third Vermouth, and one-third gin, and shake with ice. One bottle of each will make enough for 30 guests, allowing them three drinks each.

Have you tried giving a cocktail party on May Day? This can prove to be an unusual success if you use lilies of the valley as your flower theme. For such a party your drinks could be served from a table completely covered with pale-green material, or a sheet tinted pale green with a cold dye, with large bowls of lilies of the valley placed around. If these exquisite flowers appear small in scale to your table setting, try placing two tall vases full of greenery, such as juniper or cupressus, in the shape of trees at each end of the serving table and insert between the greenery tubes of water containing the lilies. These tubes can be obtained from chemists, though plastic toothbrush holders or small bottles may be used instead. This idea will give a 'lift' to these tiny flowers, and you can emphasise their importance by placing smaller bowls of them on lower tables. For further emphasis, the air can be sprayed with Muguet scent or toilet water, or, if your party is in the evening, you might try putting a few spots on the electric-light bulbs; the heat of the light will release the scent. A favourite trick of mine is to add a few drops of scent to boiling water; the steam perfumes the atmosphere.

Another May Day idea is to introduce a miniature maypole in the centre of your serving table, with different coloured ribbons leading to dishes of sandwiches and *canapés*.

During the month of May, when tulips abound, they can be massed round the house, some perhaps arranged in lined wooden clogs. When lilac appears, nothing could be more lovely than to use branches of this sweet-smelling blossom in mauves, pinks and purples, with no other floral additions. I remember visiting Lady Astor at Cliveden once during May, and seeing in one corner of the entrance hall a massed display, rising to about ten feet from the ground, of all shades and varieties of lilac. I discovered later that the head gardener had placed the stems in a series of tin tubes fixed to a frame in rows one above the other. The effect was quite devastating, but could easily be copied by anyone using this lovely flower massed in vases round the party room.

If guests are to stand, arrange the flowers on tall pedestals, or raised on boxes covered with pink paper or material, placed on the serving table. Lilac can be cut short and arranged at the top of tall candelabra, but however you use it, you may like to emphasise the pink, mauve and purple colour scheme. If your party is at night, try fixing a spotlight to focus on to the lilac (pinks show up well in artificial light, but purples and mauves are inclined to appear dull unless spotlit). To extend your colour scheme, why not cover the serving table with a pink cloth and serve pink gin or pink champagne, both made pink by the addition of a few drops of Angostura bitters?

Once you begin to think about it, the ideas for specialising are endless. I remember once trying a red theme, using flowers of all tints and shades of red placed about the house and

(Right) This buffet table decoration composed of crimson carnations and pinks allows for food to be placed under it. The green hellebores and tassels of Garrya elliptica *adds to the interest*

(Page 112) Garden flowers in the hall always spell welcome to the guest of a party in the house

(Page 113) If you live in town and have to buy your flowers, here is an idea for using white iris and yellow tulips and daffodils. Greater height can be obtained by standing the arrangement on a block

on the serving table. The only relief was given by a frill of apple-green ribbon round a posy of red carnations, which I set on a curled banister at the foot of the stairs. Flowers of all one colour are sure to be noticed and talked about, and are certain to create a greater impact than if you have vases of mixed blooms dotted about the house.

Try the effect of all-pink flowers at a Sunday morning gathering. There are endless sizes, shapes and varieties of pink flowers growing in our gardens, or obtainable from a good florist, and a hostess can gain great *éclat* by planning the flowers, drinks and eats in the one colour, using a pink cloth. Think of the delightful effect of large vases of tall pink larkspurs, shorter pink godetia, with pink sweet peas and pink cornflowers. For an important effect, the pink cleome or spider flower is admirable. Easy to grow, but unusual to look at, it always evokes a lot of comment; placed with large grey artichoke or cotton thistle leaves, it can appear magnificent.

For your cocktail party on a hot summer's evening, you might enjoy arranging all-white, or white and green flowers, for these give a wonderfully cooling effect. Bowls of green apples, dishes of green olives, cheese-filled celery on lettuce leaves, all add to the effect, which can be accentuated even further by adding green candles. On such an occasion, you could criss-cross the tablecloth with green ribbon, weighing down the ends with bunches of greenery pinned on.

Do try adding height to the top of the table by covering several boxes or tins with white or coloured paper; these, placed at different intervals and heights on the table, create a three-dimensional effect to the setting.

A winter table decoration of mimosa, freesias and single chrysanthemums, tucked into wet Oasis which fills the candle cups held by the candelabra. The candles were inserted before the flowers were positioned

BUFFET PARTY ARRANGEMENTS

Many experienced hostesses are finding a buffet party more acceptable to their friends than the cocktail party. I must admit I enjoy these much more myself; there is a casualness about them even if it is studied. As a guest you know you are not going to starve or hover from one leg to another; as a hostess you may relax in the knowledge that guests can either help themselves or be helped at the serving table and, providing enough sitting-out places are available, you or your guests may wander from group to group.

The flower decorations for a buffet table are better placed high, either an arrangement in the centre with the drinks at one end and food at the other, or a tall decoration at each end of the serving table with the food placed centrally.

I have seen a well-laden buffet table placed in front of the fire-place with decorations on the mantelshelf, and since a lot of the interest will be centred around this table the flower scheme should be well accentuated.

Piles of bread in baskets, bowls of radishes, fingers of celery and cheese straws can be placed around, although I prefer concentrating on the cheese, the wines and, of course, the decorations. The decorations, whether of fruit, flowers or gay tablecloths and candles in wine bottles, will all add atmosphere. If your setting will allow it, try to include vines or trailing creepers into your decorative scheme and combine these with bunches and bunches of grapes, together with ears of wheat and barley and bright, but not formal, flowers. Pottery, pewter and wood are ideal as containers or additions for bright flowers, such as daisies, sunflowers, marigolds, dahlias and gladioli. If your home setting is more formal, however, there could be nothing more lovely than grapes and vines and a few flowers spilling over from the rims of Dresden or Meissen china compote dishes. Candlelight, whether from candles in candelabra or wine bottles, is ideally suited to the mellowing atmosphere of a wine-and-cheese party.

For those who like curry, and there is an increasing number who are acquiring the taste for spicy dishes, nothing is more inviting than a curry party. Strings of onions, fruits and vegetables arranged together are all suitable at such a party, but the decor can only be decided after considering the background. Obviously, strings of onions would appear incongruous on a table in a formal room, but would be in keeping should the curry be served in the kitchen. Today, so many kitchens are attractive and have character, that it is becoming quite popular to eat in the kitchen after drinks have been offered in the more formal rooms. Onions, seed-heads, leaves, fruits and gourds all make attractive curry-party decorations, and I would suggest that chilled white wine, cider, beer or soft drinks be offered, since spirits are not as a rule drunk with curry.

Do make plenty of the basic curry sauce; bowls of this, placed around the room, will prove very welcome, for potato crisps, pieces of cauliflower or fingers of toast can all be dipped in it.

Many variations for a specialist buffet party come to my mind. Imagine, for instance, a party where only fish dishes are offered. This theme could be emphasised with plant or flower arrangements made in shells; fish net and scallop and other shells could all be introduced on the serving table, some of the more shallow type being used to hold tit-bits.

FESTIVE OCCASIONS

What a wonderful chance there is to show skill and expression with flower decorations when faced with the opportunity to 'do the flowers' for any special occasion. It may be a birthday, a wedding, a christening, an anniversary, Easter, Guy Fawkes or Hallowe'en, or any of the other very special occasions we are called upon to celebrate from time to time. Whatever the event, I do suggest you let the flowers help tell the story; play up the theme, even if you suppress some of your personal likes. This means that even if you are fond of pink chrysanthemums and beautiful lace cloths, it would prove more interesting if your floral arrangement for, shall we say, a Guy Fawkes party reflected this theme with more suitable material. Feature erect bulrushes to represent rockets, some of them glittered to resemble sparklers, placed as the background to a grouping of fiery-red nerines and gold and yellow chrysanthemums, balanced low down with pieces of barkwood, twigs and other items.

Guy Fawkes parties can be held in the evening for grown-ups too, although they have now become chiefly associated with the younger members of the family, and are often celebrated, as darkness falls, in the garden where the bonfire reigns supreme. A good idea here is to offer mugs of cocoa, buns and hot sausages to be eaten by the glare of the fireworks, and a lot of fun can be had from cooking potatoes in the ashes of the fire. Parents and elder brothers and sisters will call for children as the fire dies down and it is then that a hot punch can be offered to the grown-ups in the house, where the appropriate flowers will be appreciated. So when giving a special-occasion party, try to emphasise the motif with your flower arrangements; in this way the memory of the event will linger on.

A festival of harvest is another occasion

Another table design made in the circlet style. Short flowers were inserted into Oasis, the bottom half of which was covered with wax-paper. A bow of ribbon each end gave length to the design

for which many parties are given and most hostesses love this theme, for it allows plenty of opportunity to display in abundance the fruits of the garden and fields. Gay coloured flowers, fruits, berries, vegetables, grasses, wheat and barley can all be featured, and this plant material usually appears more effective when placed in brass, pewter, stone, pottery, wooden or basketware containers.

Flower arrangements for Easter festivities are usually interpreted with white flowers, so arum and Easter lilies are often used, being symbols of purity and dignity. Tall, upward-surging yet simple arrangements, signifying ascendancy, are favoured at this time of the year.

Birthday party flowers should of course compliment the person whose party it is, so flowers must be chosen to suit them and not yourself. For a demure young girl's 'coming out' party, you could try to emphasise the background by arranging large bunches of Queen Anne's lace, marguerites, pinks, cornflowers, candytuft or sweet peas, or any unsophisticated flowers in pastel tints. Tie them up with large bows of pink or apple-green ribbon; accentuate them by their quantity, for these simple flowers have no exotic qualities. On the other hand, a similar event staged for an eighteen-year-old outdoor girl, perhaps a keen young horsewoman, would call for arrangements made with branches, grasses and field flowers. If the event is more formal, try designs using more precious flowers in elegant containers.

Twenty-first birthday party decorations are planned round the theme of the coming of age. Naturally the figure '21' is emphasised on cake, candles and decorations. Cards and congratulatory telegrams can be prominently displayed and the buffet or party table flanked by large cut-out cardboard keys, a symbol (even though not always significant today) of the recipient being allowed the

Pink roses and heather with apple-green ribbon made effective decoration for a wedding table. The cavorting cherubs added sparkle to the scene

freedom of the house. The flowers on such occasions can be arranged to suit the person, or, if a girl, the colour of her dress. On one such occasion I made a tree composed of bare twigs from the garden, on which I hung twenty-one keys, all previously gilded. After the toast had been drunk and the cake cut, the young person concerned was asked to choose one of the keys which would open a box containing something she dearly wanted. To help her choose we all voiced 'You are warm' or 'You are cold', accompanied of course by sips of champagne. As

Held in a large tray, this colourful arrangement of fruit and flowers seemed ideal for a sideboard

she approached making her decision we all cried 'no' or 'take the lower or higher one' until finally she made her determined choice, and, of course, as previously arranged, it was the right key which opened the box containing a present.

When planning designs for a gathering after a christening party, rather simple flowers are called for. Choose pink or blue or pastel-tinted flowers and place them in unsophisticated vases. Many florists supply pottery or basketware cradles, which look delightful filled with forget-me-nots, polyantha roses, pink chrysanthemums and the delicate gypsophila. For your party, plan a christening cake over which hovers an artificial stork, and if you possess some porcelain figurines of storks or herons, you could hang from the beaks little bundles filled with sugar almonds. Place large bowls filled with sugar almonds around the room; in fact, as a gesture, why not do as is done on the Continent, give each guest a small bag or package containing sugar almonds, a symbol of the coins and gratuities distributed by the godfather at christenings in earlier times.

Set among candlesticks, this circlet of roses named Moonlight added to the atmosphere of a formal dinner party

A christening is not a long ceremony in church, though it is important to those who take part in it. Some people like the memory of a flower-bedecked font, but do first make certain that there is no objection to this. A delightful decoration can be made by fixing round the font a roll of chicken wire filled with moss, into which small flowers in season are inserted. Another idea is to string or wire together a number of meat-paste pots, fixing them in a circle round the font. Fill each little pot with water, adding flowers and trailing leaves.

Flowers for a wedding are quite special and come into a category all their own. Here I would like to stress the importance of contacting your florist early for such items as head-dress, bouquet and bridesmaids' bouquets. The making of bouquets is a professional job and only a professional can do it well, so, no matter how keen you are to try it for yourself, my advice is - don't. It is always better not to tread into the domain of the florist; she has gained her skill by years of hard work and practice, and she will be much more your friend should you need her help at some future time, if you leave her to do the job for which she has been trained.

Most florists will arrange the flowers for the reception and the church, if requested to do so, but if you feel you can manage this yourself and would like to do it, then there are a few principles to be borne in mind. Always consult the vicar before planning your church decorations; the church is his responsibility and he may not approve of some decorative schemes. Some incumbents do not allow flowers on the altar, some do; but in all cases if they are approached seriously and the wishes of the bride explained, they are usually most co-operative.

Flowers for the altar should not be too imposing and should be white; but yellow, pale pink or coral can be used for large pedestal arrangements for each side of the chancel steps, or you might try choosing flowers which will combine with the overall colour scheme of the bridal retinue. The bride may be wearing white and the bridesmaids yellow; then employ these two colours in your flower arrangements. On the other hand it may be an all-white wedding, with the bridegroom in uniform, in which case you might introduce his regimental colours into the flower scheme. Alternatively, keep to an all-white scheme; but always try to avoid buying the flowers without previous consultation with the bride.

A similar colour scheme to that of the flowers in the church can be introduced in the reception rooms, and an elegant arrangement of white flowers, placed on the mantelshelf or on a pedestal, will form a lovely framework for the bride and groom as they stand waiting to receive the congratulations of family and friends. As a change, I once used a white birdcage on a tall stand for a young friend's wedding, allowing sprays of pink and white carnations to flow out of it. A pink ribbon bow was fixed to the top, encircling a delicate white dove which held a ring in its beak and peered downwards. Inside the cage, surrounded by the carnations, was the bird's mate. All the guests loved the idea, and it is yours to copy.

Wedding anniversaries call for celebration parties and it is a good idea to introduce, with floral decorations, some of the symbols that are attached to these anniversaries. In arranging flowers for a twenty-fifth wedding anniversary celebration, try to introduce silver, perhaps by using white flowers in a silver bowl or vase tied with a silver tinsel ribbon. A golden-wedding celebration might feature golden-coloured flowers. There are so many in this colour range from chrysanthemums, roses, gerberas, carnations, dahlias, gladioli and day lilies. These could be placed in either a new golden-wedding-present vase, or in a vase or bowl which was an original wedding present, for sentiment's sake. Alternatively, any existing vase or basket can easily be covered with gold paint. This is definitely an occasion that should be emphasised with as much gold as possible, so buy some gold lamé or gauze and use as a table-cloth. Buy candles on which the number 50 is marked in gold. (Any good store will get these for you.) Celebrate with a cake bound in a gold frill and use gold-paper doilies. Allow the number 50 to remain prominent, even if you cut this out in cardboard and cover it with gold paint. And of course champagne or sparkling wine is a must.

So much for gold, but think of all the ideas that can be exploited when planning flowers for other wedding anniversaries. The symbols are as follows: for the tenth, tin; the twelfth, silk; the fifteenth, crystal; the twentieth, china; the thirtieth, pearl; the fortieth, ruby - what a chance here for flower displays; while, if any two people reach this blessed state, the sixtieth wedding anniversary has diamonds for its symbol. If after all this you still want to be original, we can go back to the first, second and third anniversaries which call for cotton, paper and leather respectively!

FOR TEENAGERS

Action, I suggest, is the operative word for teenage parties; it is the age when one is vitally interested in anything and everything that is happening, and keen to be doing something towards the fun. Action can start with the young people making their own party decorations, for many are more clever than their elders at devising interesting flower arrangements and clever backgrounds, their ideas usually veering towards the original. An invitation to a Valentine party, a Hallowe'en party, a Square Dance, a Travel Film party or a competition ramble will not only evoke great interest from the guests, but will also give wonderful opportunities to the young hostess or her parents to devise unusual decorations.

For a Valentine party a delightfully apposite idea would be to use hearts cut out from red art paper as a decorative motif throughout, centred with a white paper doily on which a bunch of violets is placed. Flower posies nestling in huge swirls or bows of tulle or ribbon and displayed at strategic points in the room also look very effective. Sandwiches can be heart-shaped, too - easily managed with a sharp biscuit-cutter. Other suggestions: a tray of small, heart-shaped cakes covered in pink, white, mauve and yellow icing arranged on lacy doilies and interspersed with tiny flower posies; a large iced cake, either heart-shaped or oblong, to simulate an old Valentine card, decorated with a lacy paper border and some sentimental words piped on in icing of a contrasting colour; dishes of crystallised violets and rose leaves. These can be purchased at most confectioners, but you may like to make them yourself.

Few parties intrigue the young more than a Hallowe'en party, on the eve of All Saints' Day (31st October), when witches are supposed to career round the skies on their broomsticks, guided by mysterious lights, such as Jack o' Lanterns. Although a number of the superstitions attached to this day are now forgotten, a few of the customs show no sign of dying out. One of these is the cutting out of spooky faces on the skins of marrows, melons or swedes, and placing a light inside (to frighten the witch).

These lights, spooky faces, mysterious messages, corn, wheat, yellow flowers and fruit and vegetable arrangements all accentuate the party atmosphere and a few mysterious games (such as 'murder') could be included. A cup of steaming soup, served from a black cauldron, might be given to the departing guest.

For your flowers, try a red arrangement made on a base of twisted blackened root wood, so that the flowers appear as flames, and this, with hot potatoes in their skins, nuts, fireworks and other sparkling items would provide atmosphere to the gathering.

For a square dance, providing there is room, the young host or hostess could arrange huge bunches of grasses and marguerites as the decorative motif. Waste-paper baskets covered with sheet music could hold bottles of milk or soft drinks ready to be served. Or, as milk is proving a very fashionable drink with young people, a milk bar might be arranged with various flavourings added to the milk; this could be a centre of attraction. Swags of greenery tied up with ribbon or bare branches from which hang oranges and lemons fixed with wire, apples stuck with flowers, will all give atmosphere to such a party. When dancing and strenuous games are offered the 'eats' should be fairly substantial and savoury. Items such as dips and sausages and two-decker sandwiches are always popular.

It is fun to arrange a film travel party during the winter, showing slides or films of holidays. If these have been spent abroad, accentuate the theme by introducing into your decor some atmosphere evocative of the country visited. For instance, if this happened to be Spain, use red, purple and yellow flowers in containers swathed with red satin capes, and pin a few Spanish travel posters to the walls. Figurines of bulls and matadors, if you have them, pairs of castanets, a doll dressed as a Spanish dancer - all will help to conjure up this hot and exciting country. Small dishes of Spanish paella could be served on such an occasion. If, on the other hand, an English seaside holiday is to be the subject of the party, green plants, fish-net and travel posters will give the right atmosphere, while the theme can be carried further by serving an interesting fish dish in scallop shells from a table strewn with smaller sea shells.

Garden flowers always attract at a party at home. Here a large grouping of pink and crimson rhododendrons are placed on a pedestal. Escallonia was added at the sides and back

FLOWERS IN CHURCH

Since the earliest days flowers have been used as a form of offering in churches; in fact, some years ago when preparing for a talk on the history of gardening in England, I made some research and discovered that before the Norman conquest flowers were almost exclusively cultivated by the monks to place on the altars of churches.

Today, perhaps more than ever, flowers are used as an adornment in church, particularly at times of celebration, and since more and more women are becoming knowledgeable about the art of arranging flowers, the devoted workers who give their time to 'doing the flowers' are anxious for more knowledge, since they are conscious that many in the congregation can appraise their work.

Let us admit that flower arranging is an art. It is an expression, but whereas you can express yourself how you like at home, there are certain reasons for the presence of flowers in church and these must be studied.

This large pedestal group is composed of yellow chrysanthemums and red berries with holly for height. Suitable for a Christmas church decoration

1. First they should be visible by all, not only by those in the front pew; so be bold and make the arrangement larger than normal.
2. You should study the architecture of the church. Some are modern, some Gothic, others panelled with wood. The background makes a difference to what you place before it. So if the background is dark, then light-coloured flowers, i.e. white, pale pink, or yellow, should be used, whereas, if the background is pale, an outline of darker foliage such as beech or camellia twigs, would be excellent to make a pattern, in front of which paler flowers could be used.

There are, of course, many suitable arrangements. Some churches demand a pedestal grouping each side of the chancel steps, others have an arrangement at each end of the Communion table, whilst others have a big grouping standing down on the floor. Then there are window sills, seats, fonts and entrances, all of which command flowers from time to time, but these are the problems I will discuss later.

First of all, let us take the large arrangement each side of the chancel steps. These should be placed on pedestals rather like the Victorians used for plants and, if these are not available, substitutes can easily be made by a carpenter.

Use a bowl or vase, not too deep, so that it will sit squarely and safely on the pedestal. Then, after filling this with crumpled wire netting (2 inch mesh), making sure it reaches above the rim, tie the whole thing, bowl as well, to the pedestal to keep it firm. Some arrangers can manage with crumpled wire netting only in the bowl, but I prefer to place a pin-holder underneath the wire, for this will hold the first tallest stems firmly in place.

Having got the bowl in place, almost fill it with water, for this will avoid the stems drying out while you arrange them and so help your flowers to live longer. (You fill up from the back when the arrangement is finished.)

Now back to the flowers, the choice of which should have come before the preparation of the bowl.

Having decided whether you are going to use light or dark flowers and leaves, first make a triangular pattern with the tallest and most pointed flowers. Aim high in the centre, for remember these flowers have to be seen from the back of the church.

After establishing the height and the width with the pointed flowers, strengthen the centre line with bigger, bolder or rounder flowers. Then add some leaves low down near the centre and finally fill in with medium flowers, working from the outside of the design to the centre, aiming all stems to a point beneath the tallest central stems. Make sure that some low flowers or leaves flow forward over the rim of the vase, allowing them to protrude well forward, for this will avoid a flat effect.

Some find, when making these large designs, that the flowers over-balance and either fall backwards or forwards. This should not happen if your first stem is placed centrally, but two-thirds back in the vase. The side stems should point a little forward and not flat out at the sides and when making the central line and filling in, it is better to work from the top *down* and *in* to the centre, and then *forward* over the rim, rather than tilt each one a little more forward which tends to make the whole topple over.

Which flowers to choose, is another question I am often asked. Of course it depends upon whether you buy or pick from the garden, or even the countryside, but in all cases try to pick some tall fine leaves or flowers for the *outline,* such as gladioli, michaelmas daisies, iris and pointed leaves, and some bigger flowers for the *centre,* and some medium flowers for *filling in.* Try to get some trailing ivy or other leaves to swerve down over the rim.

Many vases used on the Communion table are narrow-necked and so appear to be difficult to arrange, but I see no reason why these should not be substituted for a pair which might prove easier to use, provided, of course, that the request is made in the right quarter. However, if the narrow-necked vase is your present problem, you will find it easier to arrange flowers in it if you first insert a plastic oil-funnel in the top of the vase, filling the wider cup with crumpled wire netting or wet Oasis. A tall stem can be inserted through the wire right down through the spout of the funnel, whilst the side flowers can tilt down into the cup.

Another method is to make an arrangement in the hand, placing some fine tall flowers at the top and some shorter flowers lower down; then, after adding some leaves, wind these stems round with wire. When firmly held together cut off extraneous stems and insert the ready-made arrangement into the narrow neck, packing it with damp sphagnum moss.

At other times I have hammered a tin on to a cork and then inserted the cork into the

These identical arrangements were set in recesses each side of the altar in St. Clement Danes Church in the Strand, London

narrow opening, although if you use this method you must seal the place where the nail is inserted, otherwise water may leak.

Whatever method you use, try not to overpower the cross on the Communion table with the size of your flower arrangements. The cross is the most important item and the flowers should be subservient, in fact they should be so angled that they lead the eye to the cross. This can be achieved if you make the arrangements higher on the outside, swerving down on the inside near the cross.

If using a wider-topped vase fill it with crumpled wire-netting (two-inch mesh) allowing it to reach *above* the rim. This will allow you to place some flowers at the side almost horizontally through the wire, although you should make sure the stem ends turn into the water.

Make the outline of your design with

Members of the congregation often bring one arum lily to church as an offering at Easter time. Here you see one of two arrangements I made for each side of the altar composed of fifteen of these lilies with their leaves in a triangular pattern

fine twigs or flowers, placing the first tall stem to the left of centre (if you are doing the left-hand vase) with further stems flowing out low on the right. Fill in with shorter flowers, making sure that some flow forward to avoid a flat effect. Repeat the idea for the right-hand vase, except remember to start with the tallest stems just to the right of centre and make the low left swerve move in towards the cross.

Use light-coloured flowers on the Communion table and try not to have all the stems of the same length. Cut some of them tall, some medium and some short, which will allow you to make a better pattern. Add a few leaves near the rim, for this will unite the flower stems to the vase and so make it one whole picture.

The interiors of many churches are dark and so can be lightened by the addition of flowers, especially on the window sills. Such places are often rather narrow, so try using long, narrow baking-tins, or chicken-feed tins, which, when filled with crumpled wire netting and light-coloured flowers can prove a great delight. The tins can be painted the colour of the window sill and so appear to be part of it, but in these small, narrow tins do add some trailing greenery to cover the tin and to act as a background to the lighter flowers.

As I have said, churches vary in their styles and architecture and this is a point that should be studied when preparing the flower arrangements; but I would also stress the desirability of studying the district in which the church lies, for this will often help you to decide upon the type of flowers to be used.

For instance, a very modern church in a newly-built community can take flowers of bold strong lines, such as gladioli or arum lilies, whereas a more ornately-styled church in a settled town will demand richer flowers with more flowing lines. On the other hand, in a country church it would appear quite out of place to arrange bought, market or sophisticated flowers such as carnations, when the district abounds in wild and cottage garden flowers.

On one occasion, when staying in the country, I was asked to help with the church flowers. I was delighted to find lovely trails of ivy and long stems of cow parsley or Queen Anne's lace as well as masses of bracken and the common yellow ragwort. Of course, I picked everything the day before and placed the stems in deep water, re-cutting the ends under the water. This avoids an air lock, especially in the hollow stems of cow parsley, and so allows for a greater intake of water. Ferns and bracken must be submerged in water for some hours before being used, otherwise they will flop.

I also picked wild dock, for its tall spires are so good for height and outline, although you could use the tall rose bay willow herb as a substitute. The more I looked around the more I could see the potentialities of many of the wild flowers, but I aimed for yellow and white flowers only as I wanted the flowers to show up in the dark church.

The church possessed two large jugs which stood each side of the chancel steps, and although I would have preferred two vases standing on a plinth or a table, I set about half-filling the big jugs with crumpled news-paper, then filling up with crumpled wire netting. The paper prevented the stems from dropping to the bottom of the jug. Using this material, you could make a similar arrange-ment as follows. Fill up with water, then make the tall triangular outline of the arrange-ment with the tall dock (take off all leaves, they make the effect look untidy).

To vary the arrangement, make the height of the design taller one side over the handle and flowing down and out over the spout. This will give the appearance of both arrange-ments swerving into the centre, rather like the Communion table arrangements I have already discussed.

After the dock, follow with tall stems of Queen Anne's lace, making some stems tilt forward, then place the yellow ragwort in between, but be sure to place it a little more 'in' than the white flowers - this will give the effect of yellow 'in' and white protruding 'out', and will make the finished effect much lighter.

Ferns can be added at the back, although if they stand in front of dark wood choir pews, they will not be seen very much. However, they do give a finish to the design and help cover the wire. Don't forget to add more water each day.

Many readers ask me about font arrange-ments, and if you need them for special occasions they can easily be achieved. I am sure many readers have their own pet methods, but I have in the past rolled up a long piece of wire netting like a cigarette, in which either wet moss or wet newspaper is placed. I fixed this round the top of the font and inserted short flowers into the wet moss to make a garland.

Another way is to string together a number of meat-paste jars and tie these round the top of the font. Fill the small jars with water, then fill up with posies of flowers.

Here is an even better method of making a wreath of small flowers to tie round the top of the font. To make this, cut a narrow length of polythene, long enough to fit round the top of the font, and wrap it around pieces of wet Oasis, leaving the top free for the flowers, the lower part being covered with the polythene to hold the moisture in. You can make it stand more firmly on the font by placing two or three strips of Sellotape at intervals from the inside of the font over the circlet and on to the outside. It will then not slip about. Oasis is good for stems such as freesias and sweet peas but is not good for primroses, violets and other fragile-stemmed flowers.

I have used another method, but here the local handyman came to my rescue. He soldered together with the aid of wire a number of chicken feed tins, to make an almost complete circle. These were filled with crumpled wire netting to hold the flowers in place. I did not join the two ends, leaving this space for the vicar's sleeves to pass more easily, but I finished the two ends with bows and long streamers of ribbon. You could use either blue, pink or yellow ribbon, and I would advise that when using simple, unsophisticated flowers for the circlet, it is better that they be inserted in the wire in small bunches. Small flowers placed singly look rather bedraggled.

For a wedding you could make the large arrangements as I have already described, but do consult the bride first, for she may have likes and dislikes about certain colour or varieties of flowers. Sometimes she is only too happy to leave it all to the one who is to arrange them, in which case try to tie in with the predominating colours of the church or of the bride's and bridesmaids' dresses. If you are required to make a very large arrangement and need greater height than that of your tallest flowers, try fixing a metal florists' cone to a stick, and place the tall central flowers in the cone, inserting the stick down through the wire. Three of these in the centre will give a considerable lift to the main line in the arrangement. Don't forget to fill them with water and small pieces of Oasis and, newspaper around the stem will keep the material upright. Should you be caught without any cones, try wrapping a six inch long piece of Oasis in polythene, leaving the top open like a bag. Fix this to a stick with Sellotape and insert the flowers into the wet Oasis. The cone or bag can easily be covered with leaves or by the lower flowers. A good scheme could include alliums (onion heads), and large grey artichoke leaves. Branches of lime flowers and lilies will present a dignified sight, and any of the pale euphorbias will add a touch of distinction to most groups.

Pew-end arrangements can also be very effective at a wedding. These can be made with a pad of Oasis, covered at the back with polythene to avoid marking the woodwork. Flowers and leaves can then be inserted at all angles to complete the design, though this often looks better if the flowers do not extend too wide. Before the flowers are inserted the pad can be tied and wrapped around with green string. Long ends should be left for fixing to the pew-end. Place some fern or moss over the edges of the Oasis to avoid the string cutting through.

Trails of ivy are so good for decorating pew ends, and on other occasions I have tied a small tin cone or jar to the ends of rows of pews. These have then been filled with flowers and as you walk in the church it is a pleasure to see the end of each row of pews decorated with flowers.

In many old churches beautiful old candle sconces can be found. I am referring to the type which rise at intervals from the pews down the aisle. Circlets of flowers can be hung from these, a bow of ribbon, with streamers, adding to the effect. Alternatively, the stand could be encircled with a garland of greenery,

(Right) Against the magnificent background of the High Altar in St. Albans Cathedral, this huge pedestal group was held by wire netting over Oasis in a large washbasin-like bowl

(Page 132) On a gilded cakeboard stand, broom, magnolia leaves and poppy seed-heads (all gilded too) were fixed at one side in Plasticine to complement the hand-made golden 'angel'

finishing with a bow of ribbon at the top. As I have written, a hanging decoration over the door is another pretty sight to behold at a wedding. In addition to a potato foundation, this can be made by covering a ball of Oasis with moss, and binding this with string, leaving long ends by which it can be hung. The flowers can be inserted at all angles until the ball of moss is covered. I have seen white heather used for this, and apart from its happy symbol, it made a charming sight.

Heather is a flower I would use again round the font and for windowsills. I recall an occasion when a huge garden trug full of heather was placed on the seat at the entrance to a country church. The handle was tied with mauve ribbon, and everyone remarked upon it. I thought this would be a good idea for a wedding if small bunches were first tied and guests asked to take one on their way out.

There are so many ways of using flowers in church and so many helpers who are interested, that I am happy to notice so many church flower rotas being arranged. This gives everyone a chance and stimulates interest. Some church groups have had talks on flower arranging.

Many of these devoted church workers who are on a flower rota are reading and studying the subject too, and many have become members of the local flower clubs. They realise also the value of tidying the flowers during the week by removing faded blooms and adding fresh ones. In fact, their valued services, which I am sure are executed with love, are appreciated by all who see them, whether they are from the locality or are overseas visitors.

Here are some final hints on conditioning and choosing your flowers for arranging in church.

Pick flowers late at night or early morning when transpiration is at its lowest and re-cut the stems under water, leaving them in this deep water in a cool place for some hours before arranging them. This will give them a chance to fill up with water, so allowing them to last longer. Personally, I add a teaspoonful of Chrysal powder to the water, for this is a nutrient and definitely adds to the life of flowers.

Take off all lower leaves. There is nothing worse than dead or wilting flowers in church, so I am always happy to hear of those devoted flower lovers who re-water and refresh the church flowers, enabling them to be appreciated by visitors throughout the week.

With all flowers used in church I would say that lightness should be the aim. Try not to pack flowers too tightly and do allow them to flow. Place your first stems firmly, then walk halfway back in the church to get an idea of the height and width you will need. Never forget that all flowers must be seen from a distance, so when you are close to them, placing them in the vase, you can afford to exaggerate.

One lady wrote to me recently stating that she is making a tour of churches in England to look at the flower arrangements, so all who are helping in this way are not only deriving pleasure themselves from doing the flowers but are giving pleasure to others who see them.

(Page 133) Tall red-dyed bulrushes gave height to the Christmas arrangement of pine, holly, skimmia and carnations. All are held in Oasis on a compote stand

(Left) Yew and holly formed the background for the china figurine in this Christmas design. Helleborus niger *(Christmas roses) and cones were inserted low down in to the well pin-holder*

CELEBRATING CHRISTMAS

There is no doubt about it, Christmas is the most exciting and important time of the year. Most of us love coping with the many necessary preparations for this festival: making puddings and mincemeat, shopping for attractive cards and presents and - best fun of all - decorating our homes. And what a chance Christmas gives us to conjure up all our ingenuity in this direction: the scope is almost limitless.

I like to take advantage of all the varied greenery available, dressing it up with ribbons, baubles, cones and glitter. Cut branches of fir, if stood in a painted tin full of earth, will make a good substitute for a Christmas tree; they last well, too, for fir needles do not easily drop. If your Christmas tree is bought several days beforehand, it can be kept fresh by standing it in a bucket of water to which a proprietary brand of fertiliser has been added. When decorating a room or a hall for a party, it would be well to treat the tree and any other greenery with a fire-resistant solution consisting of a pound of ammonium sulphate (obtainable from the chemist) to two gallons of water. Spread newspapers on the ground or floor and spray the solution on to your tree and green foliage, allowing it to dry before placing it in position.

Bare twigs, ivy, holly and pine were all set in a well pin-holder on a rough wooden base, then sprayed with artificial snow. Pine cones were added and, together with red berries, two 'red robins' were fixed on a branch for extra effect

Holly, beautiful and festive in appearance, loses its leaves quite quickly in heated rooms, but it will last longer if the stems, especially at the leaf joints, are brushed over with thin glue or clear varnish. Another effective treatment is to spray the leaves and stems with hair lacquer to hold them firmly in place, or, if you want to colour them, aerosol spray paints in gold and silver will give a very gay effect. If you are using a large amount of holly, it is probably far more practical to swish the branches through a bucket of Polyfix mixed with water. This mixture is a form of size and is generally used for wall-papering, but it will close the joints and pores of the leaves, and so help your decorations to last longer.

For white decorations, using large leafless branches, seed-heads, barley, wheat, pine or yew, you will need a pail or bath of oil-based white distemper. Swish all the material through this solution and hang the items upside down to drip and dry. Silver or gold glass glitter can be sprinkled on just before the distemper is dry or, if the material has been prepared well in advance, it can be brushed over on the day of assembly with thin glue and the glitter sprinked on from a flour sieve.

White liquid shoe-polish or flat white paint is excellent for covering individual leaves such as magnolia, laurel, rhododendron and cycas, and it is useful for cones and bark when you want them just flicked with white on the edges. For a heavy snow effect on the tree, whisk up a bowl of concentrated soap-flakes and flick the foam on to the branches, where it will settle like bubbly snow and stay firm.

Children are thrilled to help at Christmas time by collecting cones, pine, nuts and other decorations. They may indeed enjoy an afternoon painting or gilding what they have collected, leaving the items ready to be assembled by grown-ups. When I was a child - the eldest of seven - we always enjoyed making animals and 'wise men' from Plasticine for a manger scene, which we constructed each year to go on a chest of drawers standing on a landing of my family home. I am sure that this simple representation of the child Christ's crib stressed the true significance of the occasion.

If you are sufficiently nimble-fingered, you can create for yourself Christmas decorations from very little natural material. You can make imitation flowers out of ribbon, dried seed-heads, skeletonized magnolia leaves and cones. These, when given a long false stem, can go to make the central interest in a Christmas arrangement.

One of my childhood memories when Christmas was spent in the country is of the paper chase always organised on Boxing Day, to which our young friends were invited. I have no doubt that it was arranged to get us out into the fresh air, but we never failed to enjoy it, returning home in the dusk with enthusiasm for the splendid tea party which followed.

You might change the decorative accent of your party during the Christmas period to suit the occasion. At a children's party the emphasis could be placed on Father Christmas, his reindeer and sleigh, the latter filled with small gifts. A Punch-and-Judy show always delights children, and coloured balloons which can be taken home afterwards are a good idea. A conjuror, or games of magic, can be introduced at parties for older children, for they love testing their own powers of observation. Fancy dress parties are eagerly anticipated, the preparation being half the fun. If a spare room is available, it could be arranged to represent the background design of Aladdin's Cave! Small presents could even be made to appear as if by magic at the rubbing of a lamp or lantern.

Family dinner parties at Christmas time are happy and intimate gatherings and although drinks and greetings will be exchanged as visiting members arrive, one of the main attractions will be the table. Take great thought for your centrepiece, which could be a tall candelabrum holding red candles and decorated with ribbon and holly, or a low design of Christmas roses and variegated holly, flanked on each side with a single yellow candle in a silver candlestick. Colours will of course depend on your general scheme of decoration, your table mats or cloth, and china. Bon-bons add a touch of gaiety, and individual snow scenes as place-name settings are original. These may be made from plaster powder mixed with water to a thick paste and poured into the lids of cocoa tins. Sprigs of greenery and small Christmas ornaments should then be stuck into position before the plaster sets firm, the name cards being added at the last minute.

I'm sure that you will find that your guests will appreciate your thoughtfulness in providing an atmosphere of good cheer that

Here is a selection of fake flowers for Christmas decorations. These may be made from ribbon, skeletonised magnolia leaves, honesty pods stuck to pine cones and teasels

This arrangement for a hall or a sideboard is made on a pin-holder in a dish, set on a base. The greenery was inserted first, with anemones giving highlight

they would not have thought of themselves, and a particularly colourful setting can be provided by burning on the fire pine cones that flare with a brilliant orange flame. The treatment of the cones is simple. First dry well in the oven, then brush over with glue and sprinkle, before the glue has dried, with chemists' calcium chloride.

An evening buffet party is an excellent way of entertaining a dozen or more friends and gives a hostess a splendid opportunity of using her ingenuity. Try covering one or more long

(Right) *This table arrangement is made with long grasses, dried leaves and teasels set into Plasticine, which encircled the candle and held it firm. All was sprayed with gold paint, and glass baubles were added for extra effect*

A tall thick candle can be held firmly by wrapping the base of it with corrugated cardboard or nylon wire pot-scourer, and inserting it on to the pin-holder

trestle tables with white cloths over which strips of wide red ribbon are laid lengthways and crosswise, as though wrapping a parcel. At the cross sections arrange sprigs of yew and ribbon bows, and to accentuate the colour scheme place candles in tall bottles filled with red-coloured water at intervals along the length of the table. A few drops of red ink will colour the water.

Christmas party settings call for special decorations. I have no doubt that each should be emphasised in one colour scheme or represented on one theme which is suitable to the background and occasion. For instance, a well-timbered old country house would be suitably decorated with fresh plant material and berries set with logs and robins, pewter, brass and pottery being the correct accessories for holding flowers, fruit, nuts and sweets. Whereas silver ribbon, glass baubles and shining Christmas trees would prove the perfect complements to a sophisticated town drawing-room. We all have our pet theories and ideas for Christmas decoration and we can all be right. The ideas which I offer are intended only to stimulate your own.

I recall one occasion when I offered to help decorate a village hall. The high walls were completely bare, so from the picture rail we hung, at intervals, long strips of wide red ribbon. At the end of each of these strips we fixed a bunch of greenery and cones at about shoulder height. To avoid monotony we then covered rings made of wire (cardboard or embroidery rings would do) with ribbon, again adding sprigs of greenery and cones at the base of each ring. These were hung in between the long ribbon strips, but ended a little higher up. Cones can easily be fixed to all sorts of bases if they are given false stems by wiring them.

Hanging wall decorations can be made by inserting pieces of yew or holly or other

(Right) Wire a ball of Plasticine at the base of the hook on a hanger; holly, yew and cones are inserted into this to make a hanging decoration

Pull out a wire coat hanger to form a circle and bind greenery to it, starting at the bottom and working up both sides

greenery into a potato. First tie round the potato with string or ribbon, leaving sufficient ends for hanging, and then insert the short stems of greenery and berries at intervals so that the potato is completely covered. Add baubles for sparkle. I have found these decorations most effective when hung in front of drawn curtains. A ball of greenery looks wonderful with a background of red curtains, and a silvered ring against blue curtains. Yellow curtains as a background for a red-and-green decoration can be the highlight of any room.

The same potato base idea can be employed for door decorations, but only one side of the potato should be covered, the other being cut flat to allow it to hang flush with the door. The longest sprays of greenery should be inserted on the outside, the cones, larger leaves and ribbon being placed near the centre.

Another hanging idea suitable for a hall is to use a wire lampshade frame, painting it white, gold or silver. Fix strands of ribbon to both top and bottom, tying the lower ones together and adding a bunch of greenery so that it hangs down. The top strands are then knotted together in a manner which will allow the decoration to be hung.

Fresh plant material is always a welcome sight, especially on the Christmas table, so try using sprays of green yew or pine with Christmas roses or red carnations or anemones. Colourful candles will add height to a grouping of short flowers. Fruit also adds a gay note to the table or sideboard. Pile into an enormous dish apples and oranges which have been flicked with egg white or boiled sugar water and sprinkled with glitter, whole bunches of grapes dipped first in beaten egg and then in castor sugar, and add coloured baubles and gold-painted nuts. The result is astonishing.

Don't forget what a valuable aid Plasticine can be. Use it in a thick ring round the top of a bottle holding a candle, inserting sprays of greenery into the Plasticine, with the possible addition of a ribbon bow. Try pressing a candle into a thick ring of Plasticine and place the whole on a silvered cardboard cake-stand.

To make a star-like base for a Christmas arrangement from a twelve-inch Polystyrene tile, bought at a household store, first mark a point halfway along each edge, two inches in towards the centre. Cut along lines from each corner of the tile to the adjacent points

(Right) To make an arrangement on the base shown above, surround the bottom of a candle with a thick ring of Plasticine, pressing this down into the tile to hold it firm. Insert the greenery and berries all round to make a table arrangement. As an alternative, with the candle omitted and a ribbon added to hang it by, it could be used as a wall decoration

(Left) Pressed into the top of an upturned goblet, a wad of Plasticine held this dry plant material which was later gilded. The candle was inserted first

A gilded azalea spray gave height to this Christmas design of yew, pine and cones, held in Plasticine on a base. A gilded wooden deer added to the interest

(Right) Another wall or door decoration made with greenery and red carnations finished with ribbon and silver 'bell'. The carnations may be inserted into potatoes

An original scheme of decoration can then be completed by inserting sprays of whitened yew, leaves, baubles and ribbon low down into the Plasticine.

Glass or diamanté glitter, gold and silver paints, coloured and flock papers can all be obtained from art stores. Candles, brushed over with thin glue and rolled in glitter, can add sparkle to dark corners.

Where space is limited, decorations based on the shape of a cone are useful. They have the advantage of being easily made in any size and in a variety of coloured materials, giving the appearance of Christmas trees. Large green ones standing at each side of a doorway are most effective, while a number of smaller ones cut from silver wrapping paper and placed over wine glasses will give a gay touch if placed at intervals along the length of a festive table. To make these cone-shaped trees you need a circle of paper, tarlatan or stiffened net. Cut the circle in half, and twist it round to form a conical shape, fixing it with Sellotape. The cone can then rest on a dowel-stick if you are making a large tree, or a knitting needle if your tree is small, and held in a tin, glass or flower pot according to size. Red art-paper cones, sprinkled with sequins and set in white flower-pots are ideal for the end of buffet tables, whereas smaller gold-paper ones, held in gold-painted tins and finished with ribbon, never fail to evoke comment.

Sequins remind me of one of the prettiest table decorations I have ever made. I covered the main cloth with tulle and lightly touched this here and there with thin glue, sprinkling sequins and glitter over it. The centrepiece was made from bows of tulle on wire stems, grouped with baubles. A frothy but altogether gay affair!

You cannot have failed to notice my particular liking for candle-light at Christmas time; its soft glimmer seems to me to spread benediction. Whether I place a large candle inside a glass globe or witch bowl, standing it in a window with blinds undrawn, or light my dining table with candelabra, I am certain to find some method of introducing them into my decorative scheme. I like to use a candle even on a landing or in some quiet corner of the room; wherever it is, it seems to give a message of peace and goodwill to all men at this hallowed time.

BEAUTY WITHOUT FLOWERS

In travelling round the country to foster and stimulate interest in flower arranging it has been my pleasure to visit new housing estates, city women's groups, hospitals, schools, hotels - yes, and even prisons! - and I have discovered that, despite our wealth of plant material, flowers themselves are not always readily available to everyone. But thousands of enthusiasts in the country have easy access to leaves, berries, root wood, branches and hedgerow wildings, while in cities many buy and carefully tend pot plants, using flowers only on special occasions. I believe that there are just as many thousands who wish to be creative with the grouping of plants, fruits and leaves as there are those who have access to, or can afford to buy, an abundance of flowers.

It brings the creative art of arranging plant material within the scope of all, for whether you are a bachelor with one branch and a pot plant or a flat-dweller with only a window-box, you can enjoy grouping plant items artistically.

A twisted piece of bleached ivy was held in the recess of this black metal container, with golden privet and ivy berries. Dried gourds were placed round the rim together with tan-coloured rowan berries

ARRANGEMENTS WITH WOOD

Wood in all its fascinating shapes and forms can be an inspiration to the flower arranger. It can be a straight, seasoned slab of wood smoothed by the carpenter and used as a base, or a slice of tree wood untouched except by the saw. It can be a twisted branch, or an eerie wisp of a dead root that will eventually give height to an otherwise low design of plants, or a piece of drift-wood which in turn has been sculptured by the winds, sea and rain. We in Britain have only recently become aware of the beauty of weathered wood but, as eyes are opened to the value of these attractive forms, more and more designers are using it, sometimes for height, but often as a dominant note in a design featuring a few flowers or leaves.

I love the natural colour of wood, especially those pieces that have become greyed and hardened by the elements. At other times, ivy roots, peeled of their bark and left shiny white, please me because their pale colouring gives a light touch to dark green leaves. Dark burls of oak are excellent when set against the light grey-green of echeverias or sedums, while burnt and blackened gorse wood will give strong line and emphasis to any lighter-coloured ferns or leaves that might form part of a design. Ordinary slices of tree wood can be rubbed with a cloth dipped in linseed oil and powdered pumice-stone. This smooths and polishes and preserves the wood. Pale woods can be stained and polished with darker shoe polish, rough edges can be sand-papered and coaxed into required shapes, whilst it is easy to fix two or more pieces together with screws or nails in order to obtain a firm wooden set piece which can dramatise your plant arrangements.

Try using wood and discover its beauty yourself.

ARRANGEMENTS WITH FRUIT

Fruit can also be decorative, for, with its infinite variety of shape, colour and texture, it offers some of the most fascinating material for the arranger to work with. There is never a time of the year when some kind of fruit is not available and, if cleverly placed in juxta-position with leaves, branches or drift-wood it can help to make most original decorations for the home or show.

There need be little waste attached to a fruit arrangement, for it can always be eaten when one is tired of the design; and when flowers are scarce it provides the best answer to the constant cry of 'How shall I decorate the dining table?'

Although it seems easier to resort to using mixed fruit, do try an all-green arrangement using green apples, green grapes and dull-green avocado pears with shiny green leaves. This would be most effective, especially if other colours are contained on the chinaware. Imagine, too, the cool beauty of a pyramid arrangement of lemons, flanked each side by lemon-coloured candles, the candlesticks surrounded low down with green leaves.

Some fruits are shiny, some have dull surfaces, some grow singly, others in bunches. Try placing the different forms, sizes and shapes in such positions that they form a pattern or design. Half fill a bowl with tissue paper or wire, then pile the fruit on top of it; on a platter set some of the lower fruit on rubber jar rings to avoid them slipping about and join other items together with the aid of toothpicks. Arranging fruit can be fun!

ARRANGEMENTS WITH PLANTS

Indoor plants, even the aspidistra, are now enjoying a revival of interest in them but the day has gone when single plants were placed in china or plastic pots and left to stand in isolated glory. Today the grouping of plants as a decoration appeals to every arranger both for the satisfaction it gives and for the beauty of the collective effect.

Three plants of the same variety set in a row have not the same decorative appeal as three of different kinds; and when choosing plants for an arrangement look for height, depth and focal interest.

Plants such as sansevieria, grevillea and croton are excellent for establishing height in a grouping, while the large-leaved *Begonia rex*, dieffenbachia and ficus will give depth. Smaller plants with variegated colourings such as peperomia, maranta and chlorophytum will add focal interest, and any trailing plants such as ivy and tradescantia are excellent for side placements and to swerve down over the container.

One of the joys of plant arrangements is that they do not demand unending attention. I find the attraction in making these groupings

This recessed shelf holds a gay plant container in which tall Grevillea robusta *is placed with trailing tradescantia, peperomia and ivy to make this home decoration*

is in testing one's ability to combine certain shapes and colours in the vast variety of containers that can be brought into use.

Old mahogany tea caddies or work-boxes look most effective when filled with plants, as do old-fashioned corner wash-stands and bric-a-bric brackets. Tankards, vegetable dishes, apothecaries' jars and wine bottles make excellent plant containers, while many of the modern vases, difficult for flowers, assume an importance of their own when filled with a single plant.

ARRANGEMENTS WITH LEAVES

During their cycle of life leaves pass through so many interesting phases in size, colour and texture that it is no wonder arrangers are turning more and more to foliage when planning their designs. Even in its dried form it is both useful and appealing. Flower club members were among the first to show the real beauty of leaves when composed into artistic designs, and often the 'Foliage Only' class at shows draws the largest number of entries.

Making a pleasing picture with foliage needs an appreciation of texture and shape. There are finy spiky leaves such as iris, gladioli, or sprays of berberis and rosemary - all so good for the main lines of a design; while for central depth or interest there are larger leaves like funkia (hosta), megasea, kale or the grey *Verbascum broussa.* These in their turn contrast with the fine lacy leaves such as *Grevillea robusta,* carrot or the grey centaurea, more suitable for dainty table decorations.

The art is in placing one texture or colour against the other; just as an artist will add a flick of white paint as a highlight and insert a dark patch for depth, so will the practiced flower arranger add a leafy spike or pale grass for highlight, placing darker or flatter leaves for depth. Variegated leaves, such as geranium, or the hardy ivy, *Hedera canariensis,* can be placed centrally for focal interest. A mixture of greys and lime green, focalised with a touch of maroon, can appear as colourful as a mass of flowers - and often more restful and cool-looking.

People living in towns may not always find it easy to obtain a variety of leaves, but a simple arrangement of ivy in a shallow dish, held down by stone chips or chunks of glass, is within the reach of all. Or try tying a few large leaves together and anchor them at the base of a fish tank, hiding the stem ends with coloured marbles. The glistening bubble effect on the edges of the leaves under water is fascinating to watch.

Foliage transpires very freely, so keep your arrangements away from strong draughts or direct sunlight.

ARRANGEMENTS WITH SEED-HEADS, GOURDS AND BERRIES

When flowering time is over, rich treasures are to be found in gardens and the countryside in the form of cones, seed-pods, ferns, fungi, seed-heads and berries, all of which make most interesting and permanent winter decorations.

During autumn many flat leaves, such as plane and elm, will press well between newspapers, while other coloured leaves like virginia creeper retain their colour if ironed between newspaper with a warm iron. The heat will cause the moisture to be absorbed into the paper and the ironing will keep the leaves flat.

Leaves with woody stems such as beech, rhododendron, *Magnolia grandiflora* and eucalyptus should be placed in a solution of one part glycerine and two parts water and left for three weeks. Once the solution is absorbed

This simple arrangement of a pine branch and colourful gourds would be suitable for a hall decoration. All are held in a bright green basket. Gourds can be grown easily from seeds

Interesting house plants are here grouped to form a decoration. Grevillea robusta *gave height with ivy and tradescantia at the sides and maranta low centre. The pots were surrounded by moss*

(Above right) These leaves were held in a Universal bowl on top of the pottery container. Elaeagnus pungens aúreo-variegata, *the gold-and-green leaf, is in the centre; the mottled* Arum italicum *flows forward low down. Ivy, aspidistra, grevillea, and camellia are other leaves used*

(Left) Wire netting over a well pin-holder held the branch of camellia leaves, whose colour contrasted with those of the fruits

the leaves will turn brown and remain permanently pliable and glossy.

Seed-heads of wild and garden flowers should be hung upside down until completely dry. This method allows the stems to dry straight. When collecting seed-heads do not forget stems of foxgloves, acanthus, cow parsley, dock, poppy and nigella. Seed-pods of regale and other lilies, as well as Japanese and Siberian iris, are also useful, while grasses and corn tassles will give added attraction to most winter dry bouquets.

Gourds grow easily from seed and once

Tall broom and yew formed the background for this grouping of decorative kale leaves. All leaves were submerged in salt water before use to avoid any cabbage smell

they are ripe they can be varnished or painted to suit your taste.

Many winter designs can be highlighted with colourful berries, and if these are brushed over with clear varnish or thin glue, they remain firm on the stems for several weeks. Place your seed-heads, dried leaves, berries or gourds in the same manner that you would living plant material, reserving the bigger leaves or seed-heads for low down and the finer sprays or grasses for height and outline. Apart from the collecting, which is both fun

This arrangement of bulrushes, dock, grasses and seed-heads was finished with bergenia leaves at the left, and was stood in a basket tray which seemed an appropriate choice for the Royal Doulton figurine

Another small ornament is used to give spirit to the windswept branch and leaves, placed behind a tree root. Tapioca in the base of the tray simulated snow

and an eye-opener at the same time, it is the placement of the different shapes and colours that makes these arrangements so fascinating.

ARRANGEMENTS WITH SHELLS AND ORNAMENTS

Nearly all shells can be used as containers, first making them watertight by painting the inside with several coats of varnish or candle wax. Left half exposed, the opening holding tiny sedums or a small succulent, the shape of a shell gives a good outline to many decorations. But it is not always as containers that I visualise the beauty of shells. Standing empty at the base of branches, leaves or plants, with the mysterious interior exposed, they make fascinating points of interest in a design. They can add texture and colour to an arrangement of leaves, just as an interesting ornament will help to tell the story of a composition.

Though some purists object to the use of ornaments with plant material, I myself enjoy their association in house decorations, provided the items are chosen with taste and used in the spirit of the design. Colour and texture should be studied, so that the ornament combines well with the plants or leaves with which it is used. One would not, for instance, surround a wooden elephant with sweetheart roses; nor would a delicate china model of a ballerina be happily placed with large ficus leaves. But the model of a heron, set in a 'pool' of water, at the side of which is a grouping of leaves and reeds, or a china cockerel dominating an arrangement of corncobs, wheat and fruit, would be entirely appropriate. The ornament must be part of the original scheme, not just added as an afterthought.

HOW TO FIX IT

The uninitiated may find it difficult to understand what goes on 'behind the scenes' to hold together the items in a design and keep the material in position. How does a large piece of wood remain erect in a shallow bowl? How can fruit be prevented from rolling about in an arrangement? How is a candle fixed upright in a bowl of flowers? The advice which follows will give you an idea of how to go about things.

Plasticine is a great boon. It will hold in place small, light pieces of wood. A thick ring of Plasticine curled round the end of a candle and pressed down on to a base will hold the candle firmly.

For an arrangement of fruit, a dome of wire netting should be made to fit into the container. Small items can be held on this with toothpicks or florist's wire, or even hairpins. Large fruits like melons may be held firm on a base or tray by placing them on a curtain ring, or a rubber preserving-jar ring.

Dry leaves and stems need support because they are brittle. Make a hairpin bend with firm wire (or use a fine hairpin), place the bend at the back of the leaf and then twist one of the ends of wire round the other, at the same time encircling the stem.

Finally, these 'tools' I have mentioned are in addition to the essential equipment I have already mentioned in chapter 1.

EASY PLANTS FOR DECORATIVE GROUPING

Asplenium nidus (Bird's-nest fern). This is a glossy green plant, very easy for indoor growing, giving long leathery leaves with wavy edges.

Begonia rex It provides gorgeous leaves of wine-red and silver, grey, purple and silver-green, all with a metallic sheen. The plant grows fast in summer, when it requires regular watering from the bottom. Avoid water on the leaves. It likes light, but not direct sunlight and needs no food and very little watering in winter.

Chlorophytum. It has thin, spiky green-and-white striped leaves and is easy to grow and care for. It will produce baby plants at the tips of leaves which can be cut off and potted. It dislikes direct sun.

Cissus antarctica (Kangaroo vine). This plant is a tall vine-like climber and is not at all fussy. You can neglect it for weeks and it will still remain green and glossy. Never overwater but it does not mind a cool spot.

Fatshedera lizei This is an attractive modern plant; it grows fairly well and has leaves like very large ivy or smaller fatsia. Green or variegated, it is suitable for a small room.

Fatsia japonica This has large, deep-lobed green leaves like fig leaves, which fall at all angles, giving a three dimensional effect. It is fast growing; likes a cool shady spot. Sponge to remove dust from leaves. Because of its

(Right) Set in a gilt urn, these maroon canna leaves give background to the green bracts of Molucella laevis *(Bells of Ireland). Dried seed-heads are placed in the centre*

(Far right) Scarlet rowan berries filled this glass jar which also held bulrushes and aspidistra leaves to form this novel decoration

bare lower stems, group it with shorter plants.

Hedera (Ivy). These are the easiest plants for beginners to grow. They like light and do not mind a cool room. Feed once a week in spring and summer but water sparingly in winter. *Hedera* Lutzii is a light and dark-green mottled variety and *Hedera* Glacier has pale-green, white-edged leaves. It looks good on its own or is useful for trailing low in a group.

Maranta. There are several varieties but the kerchoveana has bright emerald-green leaves with brown velvety spots and is very effective for the base of a grouping. It likes a warm, moist atmosphere. Stand the pot in a saucer of warm water occasionally.

Philodendron scandens This is an easy climber, suitable for training up wires or on a frame. It does not need much light and prefers a cool, sunless room, yet it will stand great fluctuations of temperature and is at home on a mantelshelf over a fire or framing a doorway in the hall. If it grows too long, you can nip off a piece and insert it in a pot of leaf mould and sand, where it will easily strike again. It has green, glossy, heart-shaped leaves.

Tradescantia (Wandering Jew). Varieties are coloured in green and white, purple and green. No one should have difficulty growing any of the varieties. It trails and is good for wall brackets. Tips can be pinched off and will root easily in soil or water.

CARE OF INDOOR PLANTS

Perhaps the best advice I can give the would-be indoor-plant arranger is not to be too ambitious at first. Many people are deterred

from keeping indoor plants because they have met with one or two failures; but it is quite possible to be successful by starting off with a few easy-to-grow plants, leaving the more difficult ones until you have become practiced. Ask your florist's or nurseryman's advice about the particular needs of the plant you are buying.

Many plants in their native habitat enjoy cool shade; others like a moist, warm but not sunny atmosphere, so in general it is important to keep indoor plants away from direct sunlight, and from draughts. But although draughts are not liked, ventilation is, so do not be afraid to open the windows so that the plants can get the oxygen they need.

Avoid sudden changes of temperature - that is, a hot room in day time and a cold one at night. See that the day and night temperatures do not vary more than 10° Fahrenheit.

Fork over the top soil now and again to aerate the earth, and remove all dead or yellowing leaves.

In spring and summer give your plants a fortnightly application of fertilizer, following the manufacturer's instructions. Keep the soil moist; how often to water can be learned only by experience. No fertilizer, and much less water, should be given in winter, the plant's resting time.

Be careful to water only from the bottom plants with fleshy leaves, such as African violets and *Begonia rex*. Stand them in a saucer and allow the roots to take up the food or moisture. Do not allow water to fall on the leaves. Hot water in the saucer will often give the necessary humidity needed by the plant.

As some plants like light, others shade, some heat and others cool conditions, it is

This purple glass model of a bird is stood in a pink and purple opaque glass dish which holds one stem of pale-green Helleborus corsicus *and pale-green grapes*

Using an ornament as a container, this donkey cart held small sprigs of berries and leaves for a dainty home decoration

better to buy a plant for a particular room, bearing in mind the spot where it will eventually stand. Most of the plants mentioned in my list are very easy to grow and most can be grouped together. If you prefer (perhaps because of colouring) a grouping of one shade-loving and another light-loving plant, arrange them together in a bowl, keeping them in their individual pots. You can remove one pot from the arrangement now and then and give it the special diet it likes for a few hours.

Picking the tips off trailing plants will make the main plant more bushy, and you can repot after three years when you think the plant is getting too big for its pot.

DRIED BUT NOT DULL

There was great excitement some years ago when I displayed on my stand at the International Flower Show in New York an orchid which had come from the top of our present Queen's wedding-cake. As the royal wedding had taken place some months before, everyone was most interested to know how the orchid had been preserved. The bloom had originally been given to a guest at the wedding, who had flown it to New York, where it had been dehydrated - or dried, in our language! - with the aid of powdered borax. This incident opened my eyes to the possibilities of drying garden material, and on my return I experimented myself and later gave a full day's talk and demonstration on this subject.

I then discovered that there is a strong fascination in drying, pressing and preserving flowers and leaves, that carried the keen flower arranging enthusiast a step further in the never-ending interest of this artistic hobby. Although we, in Great Britain, are blessed with growing material at almost all times of the year, there are many who live in towns and cities, who, when flowers are expensive during the winter months, find that a dry arrangement is a very useful standby.

Dry flowers, however, were never meant to take the place of fresh flowers or foliage, but they are certainly time-savers, for they can be prepared in advance and brought out only when needed. In most homes, there is nearly always one place where a permanent arrangement of dry material can stand when flowers are scarce or expensive. These arrangements need not be dull. Whereas a few years ago most dry arrangements were made of dried fern and seed-heads, today some of the most lovely designs are composed of dried summer flowers, the colours of which can be preserved by hanging them upside down in a dark dry cupboard.

There are four methods of preserving material, and after a little experimenting you will quickly become accustomed to using the one that suits your purpose.

This colourful yet dried arrangement was made on a pin-holder standing on a mauve china plate. The brown branch gave height and the five folded yellow hosta leaves gave outline to the two dried purple artichoke heads

THE UPSIDE-DOWN METHOD

This suits many spiky summer flowers. They should be picked before they are fully mature, then strung in small bunches and hung upside down in a dark, warm cupboard or room. When they are dried, pack them away until required in the autumn. This method leaves the flowers slightly shrivelled, but otherwise dry, and the darkness in which they are dried will prevent the colours fading. This method suits most seed-heads and sprays such as acanthus and dock, and also summer flowers such as astilbe, lythrum, delphinium, larkspur, golden rod and echinops. You may like to try others, though very soft-stemmed flowers often fail.

THE BURYING METHOD

Many open-faced flowers - zinnias, marguerites, scabious and marigolds - preserve well if buried in a box completely covered with powdered borax, or better still, the powder called silica gel. This powder is quicker in action, and the colours and shapes of flowers buried in it emerge almost life-like.

I prefer to use dried, open-faced flowers as focal interest with bare branches or bleached leaves. I do not care for a complete arrangement of dried summer flowers. They seem to look so sad. Conversely, I love an arrangement of dried twigs, seed-heads and leaves.

Using borax or silica gel, cover the bottom of a box or biscuit tin with a layer of the

(Left) Four dried onion seed-heads are here placed with dry palmetto leaves in a black metal container. Bleached ivy root encircled the stems and covered the holder

(Right) This bronze figurine held a grouping of dry aspidistra leaves with Australian gum pods and millet seed stems - all held in Plasticine

(Left) This arrangement is composed of dried fern and solidago for the outline, with dried achillea and helichrysum down the centre. Pale-green dried amaranthus (love-lies-bleeding) was added with seed-pods and dried hydrangea

(Right) This gay 'nut' tree, suitable for a celebration at any time, is composed of short sprays of pine and a selection of wired nuts inserted into a cone of wire-covered Oasis, held firmly on a pin-holder

powder. Since the stems of some dried flowers will break off when brittle, you can add a false stem by inserting a hairpin-like piece of wire down through the centre of the flower, giving it a twist under the calyx. Then stand or lay the flowers on the powder, and pour more powder all over and around them, lifting the petals now and again, so that some powder goes under and over and in between so that they retain their shape. You must leave the flowers in borax for about three weeks, taking great care when removing them, for they will now be brittle and dry. Only three days are required for flowers buried in silica gel, and as this powder remains dry, it can easily be shaken off and used again. I have dried a whole corsage in this manner and some dahlias which I dried three years ago with silica gel still look fresh and bright. Try all kinds of open flowers this way, unless they are clustered together on long stems like lupins. It is great fun experimenting. I often pull out the dead petals of carnations from the pale-green calyx. I then dry the calyx which finally looks like a small pale-green tulip. I have also dried the saucer part of *Cobaea scandens,* the pale-green climber flower which can be grown from seed. The flower looks like a Canterbury bell, and when the bell drops off, I fix a false stem to the 'saucer', dry it, and so have green 'flowers' in winter.

Dimorphotheca (commonly called Star of the Veldt) also dries well in silica gel, and I

have made fascinating dried flowers by clipping the petals of heleniums, gaillardia, rudbeckia and the other types of daisy flowers, and then drying the centre. The brown centres, with small tufts of colour, give interest to dried decorations, like so many other flowers which all emerge from their burial with new life.

THE GLYCERINE AND WATER METHOD

Most leaves on woody-stemmed branches are preserved in this way, and for those who live in towns and need foliage for the background of their arrangements, this is a good method to ensure a supply in the winter.

Wash all leaves and trim damaged or unwanted ones, splitting the stem ends and standing them at least three inches deep in a solution of two parts hot water and one part glycerine. Leave for two or three weeks until the solution has been absorbed. Of course the leaves will turn brown, but if you want a mottled effect you can remove some leaves when half-preserved or stand branches in the solution at different times of the year - for beech leaves, preserve some in August, others in September, and still more in October.

Leaves of a fleshy-stemmed nature will not absorb this solution, but others such as beech, *Magnolia grandiflora,* laurel, pittosporum, laurustinus and mahonia will take it up quite well and remain preserved indefinitely. I have fully submerged some smaller leaves such as ivy and lily of the valley, but if you want to preserve others, do try experimenting yourself.

PRESSING METHOD

Ferns and other flat-surfaced leaves are preserved by the pressing-between-newspaper method; although when dried in this manner they remain flat, some very interesting lines and shapes can be retained. Funkia leaves can be folded double and placed between sheets of newspaper, while iris, gladioli, ivy, raspberry leaves and all ferns will dry in the same way. It must be remembered, however, that the leaves will be brittle and not pliable as with the glycerine method. Plenty of newspaper should be used as this will absorb the moisture and some weighty objects such as books should be placed on the top of the pile to ensure even pressure.

The subject of drying material is a vast but very interesting one and can only lightly be touched on in this chapter, but for those who are interested I do advise you to keep your eyes open for all kinds of seed-heads and material which will make interesting lines, such as dock and dry branches. Do not forget the value of grains and grasses, whilst cones, pods, nuts, fruits, globe artichokes and gourds are excellent for focal interest.

Pussy willow and bulrushes dry well if kept out of water, and interesting shapes can be obtained with broom if you wrap it in newspaper and bend it to the desired shape leaving it to dry in this position.

Another item which attracts the keen flower arranger during autumn and winter is the dried hydrangea. These blooms should be left growing until they are fading or past their best. The colour then begins to turn, and if they are cut at this stage and placed in about an inch of water, they will slowly dry out as they become deprived of nourishment. Not all hydrangeas dry alike, so it is as well to attempt a number in order to vary the colouring. These blooms also dry well when hung upside down, but do make sure they are past maturity before picking and not, as with flowers of the

In this formal dried arrangement can be seen bulrushes, cycas leaves and glycerined eucalyptus for outline, with lotus seed-pods and gilded gourds in the centre. Skeletonised magnolia leaves and grey-green dry Ballota pseudodictamnus *lightened the effect*

delphinium family, picked for drying before maturity.

SKELETONISING

In Victorian times there was a vogue for 'phantom bouquets' and these skeletonised leaves are again returning to favour. Certainly, they give a delightful touch to a dry arrangement. *Magnolia grandiflora* leaves respond well to this treatment, although I have also tried galax and faded iris leaves, but if you wish to try these you must boil the leaves for thirty minutes in a quart of water to which a dessertspoon of soda has been added. After leaving the leaves to cool in the water, they should be spread out on paper and all the fleshy parts should be scraped off with the back of a knife, taking care not to split or tear the leaf. Then place the leaves in some bleach water and leave for an hour, finally rinsing them in clear water.

Finally, wipe them carefully with a soft cloth and then press them overnight between sheets of blotting paper or newspaper weighted down with heavy books. False stems can be wired on and, although these leaves last well and keep their shape, they appear very light and airy, and certainly give an ethereal appearance to a dry arrangement.

These skeletonised leaves can also be purchased and are a great aid if you do not have the time to spend preparing them for yourself.

Half the fun of drying flowers lies in experimenting for yourself. Dried acorns strung together can look like a bunch of brown grapes. Walnuts can be pierced with a red-hot needle and handled in the same way. Fungus can be dried; ivy roots can be stripped of their bark, then bleached and polished; pine cones can be cut to assume the appearance of a rosette; onion-heads can make a lone stand or be mixed with other items in a design; there is no end to the fun of watching the growth of flowers in the summer to see what their seed-heads will produce.

This hanging decoration can also be laid flat for a table decoration. Dried grasses, plane leaves and physalis (Chinese lanterns) were inserted into putty on a slice of wood

DRY ARRANGEMENT COMBINATIONS

Clear-cut designs and a contrast in forms of materials are two essentials for making successful dry arrangements, and although the subject is endless, the greatest interest is gained by experimenting. I hope the arrangements illustrated on the adjacent pages will give you a few ideas. But here are a few suggestions for material to use.

Some dry arrangement combinations:

Dry golden rod, glycerine beech leaves and purple statice.

Golden rod and red celosia (cockscomb).

Pink astilbes and blue delphiniums.

White statice and grey reversed raspberry leaves.

Brown iris seed pods, brown magnolia leaves and pine cones, cut in half crosswise to represent rosettes.

Dried green fern and sprays of white honesty, with dry green amaranthus (love-lies-bleeding).

Wheat, magnolia leaves and gourds for focal interest.

Lichen-covered branches, raspberry leaves and the pale-green calyx of carnations or dahlias. Pull the petals from dead carnations and the remaining calyx resembles a small green tulip, while that of the dahlia looks like a strawflower.

Wild dock, picked and dried at different stages in beige, red and brown with mauve statice and honesty clustered low.

THE FLOWER SHOW AND CLUB MEETING

THE VALUE OF SHOWS

The whole point of any visual or social art is that as many people as possible should look at it: so that for our purpose flower arrangement shows are the perfect answer.

A flower arrangement show is for everyone. Whether you are a member of a club, an exhibitor or a spectator who loves to look at beautiful things, it is a meeting ground for all who love to grow and use flowers for indoor decorations and as a means of artistic self-expression. It also provides an occasion for the exchange of ideas which will stimulate new lines of thought, and it can become an oasis to which many who are tired of the rush of the world today may come for spiritual refreshment.

Shows are of particular value to new members of clubs. While experience is gained by exhibiting, even in the novice classes, much can be learned from discussing the more advanced exhibits. At the same time the more experienced members need to compete with each other, for it is only after years of stiff competition that you will be familiar with all or most of the pitfalls, and will be able to go forward to the greater heights offered by invitation classes.

Many contend that flower arrangement, as an art, should not be competitive. On certain scores I am inclined to agree, but I am convinced that nothing which is really worthwhile has ever succeeded without competition. Competition is a spur, it urges us to do our best, it makes us try harder than we really need to; and even if we do not win, the effort will help us learn facets of the subject, which we had not realised even existed before.

It is only when all the problems of competition have been appreciated that one is fundamentally ready to exhibit non-competitively on a higher plane. Then creation rises beyond competition, as in the work of the many really fine artists we have in Britain today. In fact, opportunities must be made for this to happen, but I am sure these experts will agree that they would not have reached

Entitled 'The Wave' after Barbara Hepworth's sculpture, Mr R. Langridge of Hassocks made this interpretive design with variegated aspidistra and green-striped arum lilies, variety Green Goddess, swerving around the 'container' made of wire and plaster

this stage of full expression without the initial competition.

By this I do not mean that there should be no non-competitive work until the top has been reached. On the contrary, shows are really community affairs and the many new members of flower arrangement societies who are not conversant with the principles of competition are more likely to show their work locally in the non-competitive classes than they are in competition. For this reason I would urge all show committees to include in their schedules some classes of each, ensuring that one or more of the competitive classes for the new members are easy and uncomplicated. If encouraged at these early stages, there is every likelihood of the new members becoming the stalwart supporters of future shows. It has been found that those who *start* by doing non-competitive work are very rarely satisfied for very long, as they quickly reach a stage when they wish to know how they will fare in competition with others.

All this means that everyone must be catered for, particularly as shows have educational as well as aesthetic value. Plants can be named, advice given, help proffered - in fact there is no town so big or so small that it cannot benefit from a flower arrangement show. No art form will succeed unless publicly exhibited and acclaimed. So let your friends see what you can do. Have a show!

SHOW THEMES AND SUGGESTIONS FOR CLASSES

The problem facing most newly elected flower club committees is how to make their particular show better than the rest. This is a problem, for in the rush of freshly kindled interest, many committees try to offer too much too soon, and find that in their enthusiasm they have exhausted all their ideas and resources at once, leaving no scope for future shows.

Of course, the committees of national and area shows should use all their ingenuity each time in order to stage the most imaginative, most artistic and most educative show, for it is at these big shows that everyone congregates to be stimulated by new ideas; but my advice to most club show organisers is to concentrate on their locality, keeping the interests of the people around them well in mind.

There are hundreds of housewives in small communities most anxious to know how to make a simple flower arrangement. Please do cater for them, for it must be rather disconcerting for the newly initiated, on visiting a flower arrangement show, to be confronted with such classes as 'Rippling Harmony' or 'Cascading Analogous'. Too many advanced classes are apt to deter the onlooker. By all means have a number of interpretative classes which will stretch the imagination and skill of the advanced members: but do include a number of simple classes, even a few free-style or non-competitive exhibits, so that the general public can be attracted by thinking, 'This is something I could do'. Classes for any named position in the home will always attract the public, for they offer something they want to know about, e.g. 'An arrangement for an entrance hall', or 'For the sideboard', or 'For the window sill'. An arrangement of 'My own choice' for first year members, or an arrangement using a candlestick, a bottle, a wine-glass or a jug are others which might solve the immediate problem of many would-be competitors. Again, an arrangement of wild flowers, or one using three flowers, will help them to appreciate that flower arranging need not take up a lot of time or money.

Of course these very people we aim to attract in the beginning often become very quickly proficient themselves, and need further classes to stimulate their interest. And that is why I advocate a mixture of both, for one is then catering for the advanced at the same time as encouraging the new.

To accent a particular locality, you could have classes featuring scenes like the Sussex downs, the Welsh hills, or even the local high street - just imagine the gay colours that could be shown here with ideas of fruit designs for the vegetable shop, flowers in picture-frames for the art shop, flowers in antique containers for the antique or junk shop, flowers in a shopping basket for the grocer's, and so on. All of these ideas will cause comment in the locality and bring your show to the notice of many who might not have been previously attracted. But do tell everyone about it. Ask each tradesman to display a bill stating his shop is to be represented.

Other ideas for young clubs could be classes featuring the seasons, e.g. 'Summer Garden', or 'Summer's Roses', 'Burst of Spring', 'Autumn Glory' or 'Winter's Table'. Classes featuring special containers, such as pewter, pottery, jug, basket or wood are all easy items; even an arrangement based on an accessory will have as much appeal as arrangements accenting a certain variety of flowers.

Try a class to interpret the weather: just imagine how many different exhibits could be displayed under 'Bright and Sunny', 'Misty', or 'Windy'. 'Dull and Cloudy' could be another, whilst 'Rain', 'Heat', 'Fog', 'Calm' and 'Gales' would all draw interesting designs. Another class could be one to illustrate magazine titles, for example *Vogue, Flair, Homes and Gardens* and *Do it Yourself.* A class for British industries could well be interpreted, as well as an arrangement of flowers incorporating glass, candles, china or fabric. Many of us have either judged or shown in classes such as the interpretation of book titles, song titles, quotations, jewels, moods, trades or professions, all of which will attract the public, who love to work things out for themselves. But do remember that since flower arrangement is what we might call the end-product of gardening, flowers and other plant material should predominate in all exhibits. In fact, interest is always aroused by classes featuring one of the varieties of flowers in season, such as daffodils, lilies, delphiniums, sweet peas, irises, roses, gladioli, dahlias and chrysanthemums. To make the exercise more complete state the *type* of arrangements you want shown, such as '*Modern* arrangements of irises', '*Formal* arrangements of sweet peas', and add the words 'any foliage or any other plant material may be used'.

An overall title or theme will often attract attention to more important shows, or shows held in the midst of busy cities or towns where it might be difficult to arouse local interest. In the U.S.A. I once visited a show entitled *Through Pink to Purple* in which every exhibit was made in flowers, leaves and other plant material in colours of pink, mauve, crimson, pale-purple, and violet. 'Pink Champagne' could be one class in which pink flowers are placed in a champagne glass; 'Purple Interlude' could be another; 'In a Crimson Container' could be another, and so on. If the bills were printed in pink or purple and the stage draped accordingly, you can visualise that such a show, even if staged in other colour variations, could become the talk of the town. Why not stage a show entitled *Round the World with Flowers,* showing arrangements featuring different countries, or why not attract visitors by stating on your posters that you invite them to attend a flower arrangement show entitled *A Wedding in Dorset* or any other county or town? Classes under this main theme heading could be: The Stag Party (for men only); The Bridesmaids (arrangements in blue or pink); The Bride (all-white arrangements); The Reception (buffet table arrangements); The

Presents (arrangements made in all kinds of containers which could be presents); The Honeymoon (arrangements depicting various countries or environs where the honeymoon might be spent); The New Home (arrangements suitable for any spot in the home).

Another theme could be *Come into our Garden,* the separate classes being: The Herbaceous Border (an arrangement featuring perennial flowers); The Rose Arbour (an arrangement featuring roses); The Water Garden (an arrangement in which water plays an important part); The Vegetable Garden (an arrangement of fruits and vegetables - obviously not to include exotic or imported fruits since the title is come into *our* garden); The Shrubbery (an arrangement showing the use of shrubs and leaves); Grown from Seed (an arrangement featuring annual flowers); The Greenhouse (an arrangement featuring exotic plants); The Rock Garden (an arrangement using succulent twigs and stones).

When drawing up a schedule it is as well to remember the time of the year, your locality and the ability of your members. For instance, it is not adivsable to include in your spring show a class for 'All Foliage' just because you enjoyed the one you saw last summer. Remember there is little foliage about in the spring. Similarly, a class for variations of one colour is not suitable for a Christmas show. Although a number of ideas can be picked up from other shows here are a few, arranged in seasons, which might prove of help:

SPRING

Time of Promîse
From the Woods
My Favourite Container
Oriental Beauty (using shallow dish)
Modern design featuring blossom sprays
Time to Economise
Drifting Daffodils
Out of the Bottle (with bottle as container)
One on a Tray
Spring Quotation
Small flowers in a wineglass
Simplicity

SUMMER

Fascinating Foliage
Colour from the Garden
From the Kitchen Garden (vegetables and fruit)
As I like it
Holiday Memories
Hot Summer Day Arrangement
The Water Garden
White Wedding Arrangement
Buffet Arrangement
Pedestal Elegance
Variations on One Colour
Depicting a country

AUTUMN

Hedgerow Beauty
Harvest Home
In a Metal Container
Dare to be Different
November 5th
Blithe Spirit (dried arrangement)
Autumn Glory
Suggested by a figurine
Hallowe'en
Fruits of the Earth
Dahlia Delight
Treasures from Land or Sea

CHRISTMAS

By Candlelight (using one or more candles)
Pantomime Time
Christmas Cards
The Holly and the Ivy
For the Sideboard (flowers and fruit)
Festive Walls (swags, garlands and plaques)
O Holy Night
Red and Gold
Cinderella (an arrangement of greenery, fruit

and vegetables using kitchen container)
Party Time - The Glitter and the Gold
An Arrangement on a Christmas Wrapped Parcel
A White Christmas
You might also like to consider as subjects for arrangements: Five Finger Exercise - an arrangement using five flowers only, with any other plant material; and By the River - an arrangement featuring water.

PREPARATION FOR SHOW WORK

Most flower club members need an outward expression for their creativeness, so there is rarely any shortage of exhibitors at shows. Of course, it is generally recognised that all members should support the work of their clubs during show time, for having enjoyed monthly meetings throughout the year, it is now their turn to support the committee, exhibiting to fellow members and public alike.

This section deals mainly with the preparation for the show and the conditioning of plant material, but I feel I should add a few further reminders. Before entering, *read the schedule carefully.* Read it thoroughly. As a rule a lot of thought and work has gone into its production in order to make it interesting to you and to the public it tries to attract. If there are items you do not understand, write to the secretary at once. I receive hundreds of letters each year, even some from abroad, asking me if I would clarify certain statements in their schedule. Only those who compose the schedule can give the answer, so do write to them and make sure you are clear about what is expected of you. If you think there is some ambiguity which might be interpreted by the judges in any way other than yours, do not worry; just as you will have checked with the committee, so also will the judges, who on discovering the misleading words will either write to the secretary or confer with her on arrival. So if you clarify the position with your local secretary and all others play their part accordingly, all should be well. The problem can then be better resolved the next year.

Mrs F. E. Allen of Whitefield was a prizewinner in a 'chrystal clear' class with this enchanting arrangement in white, pink, blue and green. The pale china-blue climber at the left is Tweedia caerulea

Choose to enter only those classes you feel confident of being able to complete and do not choose too many, unless you are very experienced and have already been able to gauge the time needed to complete them all. Your best work will evolve if you have time on your hands, whereas if you are trying to complete a number of arrangements and

'Ancient Treasures' was the title of this dry class in which Mrs D. Wolley of Ferring, Sussex, won a first prize at a N.A.F.A.S. festival

working with one eye on the clock, your work is sure to become a little mechanical.

Make sure you have all the equipment you will need. It seems almost unnecessary to add this; and yet I recall an agonised moment for a competitor in one of the big northern shows, who discovered she was short of one pin-holder which she badly needed for a modern design of chrysanthemums. No one had an extra one and no shops were open, but after thinking of all kinds of substitutes, none of which would work, I thought of the horticultural tent where the vegetables were being staged, and there obtained a large potato for her. This was cut lengthwise to lie flat on the dish and holes were made in it with a pencil, allowing the competitor to insert her flowers and complete her design, which delighted the judges sufficiently to win the second prize. *But,* it was a harassing time for all, and there might not have been a horticultural tent nearby. So do check on all your needs, taking extras in case of accidents. Items necessary may include pin-holders, wire netting, reel wire, conical tin tubes (for mass or pedestal groups), glass orchid tubes (for short flowers high in a design), modelling clay, rubber rings (to avoid holders and fruit from slipping), Twistems (to steady heavy branches at the back of tall containers), flower scissors, mist spray to moisten the surrounds of your exhibit, tooth-picks (for fruit) and a long-spouted water-can. Chrysal powder (to keep flowers living longer), Sellotape, drawing pins or paper clips or stapling gun (for drapes), boxes (on which to stand exhibits for extra lift), and Stemfix or Oasis may all be used. Pieces of strip lead may be needed to hang on the wire at the back if your arrangement is inclined to tilt forward, though it should not do this if properly constructed. Take a bucket for water and, of course, the necessary containers, bases, backgrounds (which should be wrapped round newspaper or on a roller to avoid creases) and accessories, to which will be added, on the day, all the flowers and plant material.

Plan your arrangements well in advance. You cannot always decide upon the flowers you might use, for the weather and market fluctuations will have to be considered; but you can make a rough sketch of the sizes and shapes of flowers you will need to enable you to create the design you have decided upon.

Containers

Next the container. If the height of the background niche is to be three feet, to achieve good scaling you will need to make your arrangement about 2 feet 9 inches high, including container. This would allow for your vase, if an upright one is used, to be 11 inches high or slightly more; therefore if your chosen vase is shorter then this you might need a block or base or even a tin or box on which your arrangement can be stood. These items can either be specially made, painted to match the container, or covered with a swirl of material. If placed underneath your container this material acts as a base which in judging is considered as part of the arrangement and not an accessory, as back drapes are. If you are using a shallow container then you should choose plant material that will give you the necessary height of 2 feet 9 inches to fill the prescribed niche of three feet. The colour and texture of your container should be chosen with care.

Drapes

Do check if these are allowed, and if you choose to use them study the effect of their colour and texture, for both will effect your arrangement. If your arrangement is mostly shaded, use a tinted background to throw it into greater relief; on the other hand, if you have made your design using mainly light coloured plant material, add a shaded background so that the highlights will be noticed. Similarly, the overall effects of your design can be enhanced by using certain textures of material. For instance a shiny-surfaced drape is often better placed with dull-surfaced plant material, whilst linen, rep and other dull-surfaced backgrounds will give stability to arrangements of lighter textured flowers. Wild flower arrangements, those featuring fruits and others of country atmosphere require backgrounds of coarse material, such as hessian, hopsack and other heavy weaves, but in the main follow the principle of light behind dark, and dark behind light. If you make an autumn arrangement featuring wheat, beige-coloured chrysanthemums with yellowing leaves and gourds or quinces, composing this with a background of natural-coloured hessian, the outline of your arrangement will be lost; whereas a brown (I think I would use a cinnamon brown) would place the complete design in stronger silhouette.

Avoid patterned backgrounds, for unless you are keeping to one colour scheme, such as pure white flowers in front of a green, white and gold embossed back drape, the patterned drape might be confused with the flowers in front of it. Net, as a background, is almost too sheer of texture to be of any value, except perhaps when used in compositions illustrating champagne, ballet, or other such themes. The vast subject of the use of drapes is interesting, for sometimes the best use of a background can be the judge's deciding factor between two equally good arrangements. The colour and texture of woven-material bases is equally important. I recall a most beautiful arrangement of maroon and mauve flowers, with maroon-coloured *Prunus pissardii* and reddish-purple *Begonia rex* leaves. All of this was in a dull pewter container standing on a grey material base. As I analysed the design I could find no fault with it, yet I could not at once discover why it had not struck me more forcibly at first sight. I took it apart point by point and tried to discover some note of distinction, without success. I was concerned, for it was quite one of the most lovely arrangements I had seen for a long time. After more consideration I finally concluded that, had the material base been of a pale mauve or lime green or even shiny crimson colouring, the design would have been lifted right out of its monotone bracket into one which could not have been resisted. The complementary colour to reddish-purple is yellow-green, and since the reddish-purple in the arrangement was shaded, it would have been better to use a tinted yellow-green for the base, or, if wishing to keep to the colour shade, a shiny crimson.

Bases

Bases can be made of a number of materials (see Definitions, page 184) and if used correctly can often help establish the balance of a design. Sometimes when a thin-stemmed plinth-like vase is used, the mass of flowers above it gives an over-balanced effect. Balance can be restored by standing the vase on a base, making sure, in good show work, that the base is in keeping with the vase and flowers above it. An oblong base will often aid a tall vertical arrangement; a tall thin design placed in a prescribed niche might leave the niche half empty, whereas if it were placed on a base the setting would become more complete, since the base is judged with the arrangement. These are all possibilities and there are no static rules, but a good experienced judge will notice these subtleties, especially in first-class show work.

Accessories

These items are discussed in the heading on interpretive compositions, so whether you take them to the show or not depends upon the classes you have decided to enter; they should be kept within the spirit of the exhibit and be of correct size, colour and texture.

Plant Material

There are many methods of getting your plant material to the show-ground or hall, depending upon the length and method of your journey. However, after conditioning your flowers and other plants, it has been found excellent for long journeys to pack everything in a plastic-lined flower box, rather close together to stop them moving about. Tissue paper can be slid around precious blooms. Place long leaves at the bottom, followed by tall flowers, shorter flowers being placed near the ends of the others together with any shorter leaves, and special ones can be packed in a plastic bag. Cover the box with more plastic sheeting and tie it down. Place the flowers in a bucket of water on arrival at the show and give them a deep drink. Another method, better for shorter car journeys, is to place most flowers in a polythene bucket containing a little water, then pull a plastic bag over the heads of the blooms, tying this down firmly to the bucket to avoid loss of moisture. Fill the bucket with water on arrival to give the flowers a long deep drink.

Conditioning of Cut Plant Material

Much has been written on prolonging the life of cut flowers and much of it is merely confusing, for long passages on temperatures and the effect of certain chemicals are mainly intended to apply to commercial growers. Folk lore has also conveyed to us the advantages of using such ingredients as vinegar, peppermint, wine, acid, tea, copper pennies and aspirins, but few of us connected with show work and dealing with mixed flowers would have time to work out what ingredient goes with which flowers, however effective it proved. Nevertheless, a great deal of help can be given to flowers by proper conditioning (see page 23), and I have found certain flower preservatives now on the market very helpful, except in the case of flowers which ooze a sticky substance, such as daffodils.

INTERPRETATIVE COMPOSITIONS

Let us admit that the exhibits that often draw the most comment from members and visitors alike are those to be seen in interpretative composition classes. Yet many newcomers to the art of flower arrangement are mystified as to what exactly constitutes a composition and what makes it interpretative.

A composition is the grouping together of certain items to make a pleasing overall picture. Without perhaps realising it, you 'compose' the items of furniture in a room; you also 'compose' the setting of a table or the items on a mantelshelf, placing perhaps a tall vase or candlestick on each side of a mirror or clock in the centre. If you place both candlesticks on one side, leaving the other side bare, the composition on the mantelshelf would appear unbalanced. So, in flower arrangement composition work, you are aiming to compose a number of items, including the flowers, into a harmonious whole to fit the space stated in the schedule. Your items may be one flower arrangement with back drape and two accessories, but in order to compose these items harmoniously the eye should be able to travel from one item to another without any jarring. Hence the reason for an appreciation of rhythm (see Definition, page 189).

To interpret, you must have a theme in your mind first.

As a rule, the schedule will give you the initial overall idea, which in turn should stimulate your own thoughts. If you find it difficult to make a start, I would suggest that you write down on paper all the things that come to your mind as you think of the title of the class. Let us imagine that you have decided that you would like to enter the class entitled 'Book Titles'. Sit down and think about all the books you have read or known, and at the same time visualise all the plant material which might be incorporated to help you illustrate the meaning of the book. I emphasise thinking of the plant material early, for this should predominate in the final picture, and it would be useless dreaming of all the things you could include in your composition which might interpret shall we say 'The Corn is Green', if the show is at a time of year when you cannot obtain corn. Of course there may be other more subtle ways of interpreting such a theme, but I am writing more of the obvious at this stage.

Having decided upon the title of the book you wish to interpret, you must gather together, even if it is done mentally, all the items you *could* include which would help to illustrate your point. It may be that the colour of your flowers will help; perhaps the container or the background will add to your interpretation. You may have just the right china figurine to add as an accessory, or a book, a statue or a pipe. Once you start thinking, many items will crowd into your mind and you will begin to wonder how you will compose them.

Do remember that only one of these items can become the focal interest, the others should lead to and from it, or at least be placed so that they are subservient to the main object of interest. Let us imagine that at a Christmas show you have chosen Shakespeare's *A Winter's Tale.* You have perhaps chosen this because you have a small statue portraying Shakespeare sitting in a chair reading, and also because you thought that bare branches would be easy to obtain and appropriate for the winter. You begin to visualise how you will compose this and decide upon a tall branch that will fit into the three foot high niche. You then decide to whiten the branch with plaster powder to give it a more wintry effect, and finally in order to give width low down to this tall bare branch, you decide to place it in a long base or dish which you might whiten.

Yes, the idea is coming and you can hardly wait to do it. You imagine you could include a book of Shakespeare's plays opened at the appropriate page; and you have some large pine cones which if whitened would add to the effect. You also have some greenery, some spectacles for reading the book (you think) and a host of other things. Stop! Now is the time to decide which one of these items is going to be placed at the foot of your tallest point to become the focal interest, and to which all other items will lead. Shall it be the book, the cones, or the statue? Perhaps you decide to place the open book at the base of the branch and the statue slightly to the left. This I would say divides the interest and is not so good, and in addition I think the open book would become too dominant.

On thinking the matter over, I feel a better way of handling this would be to place the tall whitened branch on the whitened base and insert some tallish green pine sprays for transition. Then at the base of the branch I would stand the whitish model of Shakespeare and make this your main interest. A few small cones could be placed around the base of the statue between which small pieces of green pine could be interspersed, for otherwise the white statue on the white base would not be thrown forward sufficiently. Then, should you wish to emphasise your meaning by adding the opened book, it could be placed *behind* the branch in the niche, so that it is only half seen. This makes it less obvious and adds a third dimension, and it could even be stood on a further pile of books to make it higher. But at least in this way you will have concentrated your main interest in one spot (i.e. around the base of the tall stem) and the onlooker's eye will be able to travel down from the top tip of the branch on to the greenery for transition, then to the figure for emphasis; then drifting off again with low trails of greenery which completed the rhythmic movement of the whole design. In other words, you have made a rhythmic composition properly scaled to fit the niche, which illustrates your meaning and which, because it is not too cluttered, will attract the judge's eye.

This brings me to emphasise the fact that all interpretative work must 'speak'. It must tell its story to the judge, for the judge's reaction will depend a lot upon whether the exhibit is quickly recognisable. A title may be added to help illustrate the meaning of your composition.

Thus the main points to consider in an interpretative composition are that it should have appropriate height and width, dominant interest, rhythm and balance, appropriate colouring and a third dimension, and that everything, including the accessories, should be suitably related. An accessory placed at the back of a niche is made to appear smaller and less obvious, one placed forward will seem to increase its size. Items recessed will give depth, whilst fine items placed protruding will add highlights.

Once a start has been made on interpretative work, it becomes a deep and abiding interest, often being carried into the home. It stirs the imaginations of all who see it, provoking others into trying it themselves. The organisers of art exhibitions have often expressed surprise at the great numbers that flock into flower arrangement exhibitions, whereas only relatively few find their way to other exhibitions. It is because anyone can arrange flowers. Anyone can obtain a few flowers which, with a little imagination combined with an accessory, can make a picture.

I wonder how many recall the Coronation Flower Arrangement Exhibition in London in 1953 which included an interpretative class representing the countries of the Commonwealth? Fearing that these ideas were too advanced at the early stage of the progress of our clubs, I was invited to give an explanatory talk to the exhibitors. I found that to interpret a country of the Commonwealth appeared too difficult, so I threw the meeting open and asked exhibitors to answer what came into their minds when I called out a particular country. 'Jamaica,' I excitedly cried, and the answer after some hesitation came back, 'bananas', 'coloured cottons and coloured people'. Good, a start had been made. 'Please,' I then went on, 'will someone do an arrangement of bananas perched perhaps on the head of a statuette of a coloured woman? Add a

check cloth, if you like, but do it!'. It was fun, we went on to Australia with coral and shells; to Guernsey with fruit and vegetables; to India with red flowers, saris as a background and perhaps a black ebony elephant. We went to Ceylon with a pool and lotus flowers, to South Africa with proteas and exotics. In fact, so fast were the ideas coming that in the end we wished for more countries. The show was a huge success, thirty-eight countries were represented, and we all thoroughly enjoyed it. It was just getting the start that was so difficult.

When interpreting items such as metals, fabrics and jewels, colour and texture are very important. For instance, sapphire is glittering and sheer, whereas jade is heavy and opaque. The former could be illustrated with delphiniums or other fine blue flowers in a blue glass container, whilst green succulents could be incorporated with an opaque container for the latter with the addition of a jade ornament, or even one carved from a piece of green soap.

Almost all classes which bear a title are interpretative. For instance, if you enter a class for a table design for a special occasion and you decide to make *your* special occasion your son's 16th birthday party, it would be much more interpretative of the occasion if you made a flower design in school colours, or used a tankard or pop bottle as a container. You might be a person who loves pink and blue flowers, and you decide to arrange these on one of your lovely lace cloths, but in interpretative work you must submerge your own likings and do something appropriate for the occasion, or else make the occasion fit your own tastes by, in this case, naming

Mrs W. Simpson of Stoke Poges made this effective design of dried material, sprayed with bronze paint over blue paint then glittered, to win a prize in a 'pleasure of giving' class

your table 'Teatime with me'. In an interpretative class for 'Moods' you might choose 'Happy' or 'Doldrums', 'In the Blue', 'Gay' or 'Jealous'. Just imagine the great varieties of colour and textures and accessories which could be brought into play.

Then, endless ideas could be used in a class which asked for the interpretation of a quotation. Think first of its meaning, then of the flowers and other plant material, their colour, size or shape, which will help express this meaning.

I wonder how many readers remember the array of thirty-two interpretative exhibits featuring Shakespearean quotations which were shown at the charity show in aid of the Gardeners' Royal Benevolent Society.

One in particular remains vividly in my mind. It was composed of a gnarled bare branch, rising from a shallow dish filled with moss and fungus, surrounded by a swirl of grey net rising high at the back. The quotation was:

'I saw old autumn, in the misty morn,
Stand shadowless, like silence listening to silence.'

As you gazed at it and read, you felt you had to creep away in case you spoiled the silence. Yes, interpretative work is fascinating and it is also very rewarding, for most competitors find that the mind is widened and extended in searching libraries, museums and other places for background information.

DEFINITIONS

Most newcomers to show work find it rather difficult to understand the meaning of certain words, phrases and regulations that are so often included in the making of a schedule.

I am in full sympathy, for I often ask myself whether it matters if a bulrush is called a flower or not, as long as it appears just right for the arrangement which is being made. On the other hand, I know only too well that in order for the great numbers of enthusiasts now practising show work to bring some basic understanding to the subject, there must be some method of defining these working phrases.

It is hoped, as we progress, that the schedule makers, especially those of newer clubs, will become more experienced and not lay too many unintended traps for the competitors; but in order to help those who wish for some clarification of the terms in use today, I print in alphabetical order a list which is in general use. That some will outlive their use or others be added in time, I have no doubt.

Accessory Any item such as a plate, ornament, book, back drape, etc., and any secondary placement of plant material which is used in addition to the main flower arrangement. Stones, shells, marbles and similar non-plant material are considered to be accessories *unless otherwise stated* in the schedule.

Advancing colours See Colour Definitions, page 190.

Analogous colours See Colour Definitions, page 190.

Annual A flower or a plant that completes its cycle of growth in one year. A hardy annual is grown entirely outdoors.

Arrangement This means the artistic use of plant material, with or without accessories, in any stated or unstated container with or without a base.

Artificial Artificial, plastic or dyed flowers are not allowed in competitions unless stated.

Balance This can be asymmetrical or symmetrical, but should have visual equality each side of the axis, focal point or imaginary central line.

Base An item on which a container can be stood, e.g. wood, metal, fabric, china, plastic and slate, or any other material.

Basket A basket could have a handle or lid and should be made of any natural woven

material unless the schedule states otherwise.
Best in the show An award given to the best of all the first prize-winning exhibits.
Biennial This describes a flower or plant which completes its growth in two years.
Bloom One flower or opened bud borne on a single stem, e.g. carnation, dahlia, tulip, scabious.
Bowl A bowl is a receptacle having a wide opening, the top diameter of which is greater than or equal to the height. It must rest on the table or be raised by a base not more than one third its own height. Unless otherwise stated, it is assumed that a bowl shall be viewed from all sides.
Bud An unopened bloom not showing colour.
Bulrush Whether it is a flower-head or a seed-head depends upon the stage it has reached when it is used. When tight it is usually termed a flower.
Candle This is considered an accessory, unless otherwise stated. Often used for colour and height in certain designs.
Catkins Hazel catkins are collections of the male flower of the catkin.
Cluster This is several fruits, berries or flowers growing close together on one stem, e.g. currants, tomatoes, grapes, phlox and climbing roses.
Colour Colour should be used to interpret adequately the meaning of the class. Leaves should harmonise. Stems and stamen colours are ignored. See Colour Definitions, page 190.
Complementary This is something which serves to complete. The lid of a container, or a tray, for instance, is complementary to the whole.
Complementary colours See Colour Definitions, page 190.
Condition This means the actual quality of the plant material at time of judging.
Container A receptacle in which flowers are exhibited. Can be made of any material, be of any texture, colour, shape or design which will enhance the beauty of the plant material arranged therein.
Contemporary Existing as of today.
Contrast This is a set of two things juxtaposed to accentuate their differences. To show a striking difference by comparison.
Cool colours Those which come in the range from green to blue. (See Colour Wheel, page 191.)
Design An overall plan which is made pleasing by the combination of all items used. It includes balance, rhythm and scale.
Distinction This is something above the ordinary yet not bizarre, notable for creative use of plant material. (See page 191, Hints for Judges.)
Dominant This term in flower arrangement means something eye-catching - something strong, influential, outstanding and overlooking other items.
Drape This is a piece of fabric or other material used behind an arrangement to give height, colour or accent, or used in a niche to emphasise the spirit of the exhibit. Small pieces of material placed under an arrangement are termed 'bases'.
Dried plant material This may include any dried, preserved, pressed or skeletonised natural plant material; also dried fruits, seed-heads, nuts, cones, grasses or sedges, in fact anything which at the time of use is not living. Generally this does not permit painting or dyeing or the use of artificial material.
Driftwood This is a wide term but covers wood which has been weathered by any of the natural elements, i.e. air, earth, fire or water, or that which is dead, dried, stripped, sand-blasted or polished.
Exhibit This means an entry placed in a flower arrangement show. It need not be in competition.
Exotic When referring to plants, this means introduced from hot countries and nurtured in Britain in greenhouses. Many now grow

happily outside, but the term 'exotic' generally refers to greenhouse plant material, and not outdoor-grown garden material.

Floral This is used to cover arrangements including all kinds of vegetable matter.

Floret This is a singly formed flower which is one of many on a spike, as found on delphiniums, gladioli, acanthus, phlox, lilac, etc.

Flowers When a class refers to the use of a certain number of flowers it means blooms or opened buds borne on a single stem, such as carnations and tulips. A spike, such as a gladiolus, is now included in this definition.

Focal point This refers to the heart of interest in a design; the point where all stems unite, usually found at the base of the tallest or main stems.

Foliage This is the leafage of a plant. Succulents and some bracts come under this heading - also stems bearing leaves. A class for 'all foliage' can be of any colour.

Forced This refers to plants brought forward, often with heat under glass, to produce blooms out of season.

Formal This usually means a conventional arrangement, which is regular and symmetrical, in a suitable container.

Fragrance This is a quantity of odour which can be appreciated. Used in some classes, particularly those for the blind.

Fruit In horticultural terms usually this means the nuts, berries, seed-heads, gourds and cones of fruiting plants. Generally, whatever develops from a flower is a fruit. In flower arrangement shows also included are edible fruits such as apples, pears, cherries, bananas and grapes.

Genus Botanically this means a classified group of plants such as dianthus which contains all the pinks and carnations and includes all other species of such a group. The plural of genus is genera.

Grasses Since few can distinguish when grass is in seed or flower the term 'grasses can be included' is added to schedules if they are needed, unless 'any plant material' is stated, which of course would include grass.

Green An 'All Green' class allows the use of any green plant material - i.e. foliage, fruit and flowers, etc. But it must all be green, not variegated. It is better to state on the schedule 'all green, any plant material'.

Hardy flowers This means all flowers whether grown from bulbs, corms or herbaceous plants which are grown entirely in the open.

Harmony This means that no one part of a design is developed at the expense of another, all elements fitting together without jarring: a unity, a consistency of likeness.

Highlight This is a fine touch, a light note, a light-coloured flower, leaf or grass which attracts the eye before other features in a composition.

Holder This is a device for holding material in position in a container.

Hue This is another term for colour (see Colour Definitions, page 190).

Informal This means a casual type of arrangement, not conventional, using a simple type of container.

Kind This applies to separate genera such as roses, chrysanthemums and zinnias, e.g. using any kind of rose.

Line In flower arrangement this means showing strong linear pattern or outline, using a minimum of plant material so that line is not obscured.

Mass This is a massed overall design using

This interesting all-green arrangement was made with garden material planted by Waterer. It shows Elaeagnus pungens aureo-variegata *placed for height with witch hazel and tassels of* Garrya elliptica *for width. Pale-green flowers of* Viburnum opulus *(guelder rose) were placed centrally with* Helleborus corsicus *over the rim. The skimmia with reddish flower heads is Waterer's Bronze Knight*

plenty of plant material and showing no particular linear shape.

Miniature Up to four inches is the usual overall size for a miniature arrangement. Fundamental rules of design prevail, but scale is of great importance. Tiny flowers, grasses and leaves should be used so that if magnified ten times, the whole would still be in proportion. Overall size includes vase and base. State size needed on a schedule.

Modern Modern designs are recognised by clear-cut plant forms and bold colouring. Contrast of textures is a distinguishing feature. Dramatic lines are used to contrast or blend with modern decor.

Monochromatic See Colour Definitions, page 190.

Moribana A Japanese term to represent an arrangement in a shallow container.

Nagiere A Japanese term to represent a free or 'thrown-in' style of arrangement in an upright vase.

Neutral Grey is considered a neutral in flower colour classes. Pewter vases have a neutralising effect.

Niche This is a space backed with cardboard, wood or other material to form a recess in which an exhibit is placed.

Originality This is recognised as the verve with which unusual plant material is used. An unusual vase, colour or style can produce originality.

Perennial This is a plant that lives, blooms and sets seeds for more than two years.

A triangular mass arrangement was made with these flowers all picked from the herbaceous border. Sidalcea, erigeron and salvia were used on the outside with monarda in the centre and pale-mauve galega flowing forward at one side and green heads of Sedum spectabile *at the other. The red* Achillea kelwayi *can also be seen low in front*

Period When exhibitors are asked to portray a particular period, such as Victorian, Georgian, *avant-garde* and modern, flowers illustrative of the period should be used.

Point system This is a system of assessing the value of a flower arrangement by giving points to various principles. Not favoured by artistic judges.

Predominate In classes where one colour or one kind of flower must predominate, this means that the particular colour or flower must be the stronger or be superior in quantity to the rest of the materials used.

Primary colours See Colour Definitions, page 190.

Proportion This is the relationship of one part of an arrangement to another, be it flowers to each other, flowers to container or the whole to background. An arrangement one foot high would be out of proportion in a three-foot niche. Proportion is similar to scale.

Recess To recess a flower or leaf is to place it in more deeply near the wire, to contrast with another which might protrude, thus giving an 'in and out' uneven effect.

Receding colours See Colour Definitions, page 190.

Rhythm Rhythm in a flower arrangement is usually created by the use of graduated sizes, repetition and transition without monotony, to give movement.

Scale See Proportion

Secondary colours See Colour Definitions, page 190.

Sedges Grass-like plants which grow in marshes or by the waterside.

Shade See Colour Definitions, page 190

Space Whether a niche is provided or not, this means the given space in which an arrangement must be placed. No exhibit should extend the given space or touch the sides of a niche.

Species This is a plant form found in nature - not produced by man, as is a hybrid.

Spike This is applied to a flower structure with short-stemmed flowers attached to a single unbranched stem e.g. gladiolus, and delphinium.
Spray This is a part of a plant or shrub bearing a number of flowers on one stem, such as solidago and forsythia.
Still life An arrangement with other objects, such as fruit, books and upturned pottery, designed to make a composition or picture.
Subservient This is an item less important than the others in a flower composition. It is useful as a means of relating one thing to another, but plays no important part.
Texture The tissue structure of plant material may be smooth or rough, dull or glossy, fine or heavy.
Tint See Colour Definitions, page 190.
Transition This is the change or passage from one item to another in a flower arrangement, often gradual in a mass style, and good transition can give movement in a curved style.
Variations The word variations (of one colour), allows for the use of tints and shades of its analogous neighbouring colours.
Variegated This means plants marked with irregular patches of different colours, mostly referred to in leaves bearing markings of white, cream or yellow.
Variety This means a named species, hybrid or other development of a genus, such as *Achillea* Gold Plate. Achillea is the name of the hybrid plant whilst Gold Plate is the name of the variety.
Vase A container which is taller than the diameter of the opening at the top. A word now being superseded by container.
Warm colours See Colour Definitions, page 190.
Water Do not forget to put it in your container.
Wire Wire netting used as a support should not show. Wiring of stems is not allowed.
X is for xeranthemum, a hardy annual with everlasting composite flowers.
Y is for you and your good efforts, which are required at every show.
Z is for zeal used in advancing the cause of good flower shows.

These definitions should be regarded only as a guide but, in order to meet most contingencies, I advise schedule-makers to add the words 'any plant material may be used' as this covers such items as bracts, spathes (i.e. arums and anthuriums) and fungus (neither flower nor foliage) which are difficult to classify.

COLOUR DEFINITIONS

Colour
Colour appeals to our senses so use it to interpret your feelings. Do not use different colours in equal amounts: strong colours are better used in smaller amounts than the more neutral ones. White, which is considered as a colour in flower arrangements, tends to absorb colours near it, while black makes them more brilliant; grey is regarded as a neutral colour.
Primary colours
These are red, yellow and blue
Secondary colours
These are green, violet and orange
Tertiary colours
These are yellow-green, blue-green, blue-violet, violet-red, red-orange and orange-yellow.
Advancing or warm colours
Numbers 9 to 12 on the colour wheel.
Analogous colours
These are tints and shades of colours lying adjacent to each other on the colour wheel, i.e. numbers 1 to 4 or 9 to 12.
Complementary colours
These are colours that are found opposite each other on the colour wheel, i.e. numbers 1 and 7 or 5 and 11.
Hue
The name of a colour, i.e. a hue of red.
Monochromatic harmony
The tints and shades of any one colour.

Receding or cool colours
Number 2 to 5 on the colour wheel
Shade
A darker version of a colour
Split complementary colours
These are one colour and the two adjacent to its complement i.e. numbers 1, 6 and 8, etc. on the colour wheel.
Tint
A lighter version of a colour
Tone
A dulled or greyed version of a colour
Triad
Three colours equidistant on the colour wheel, i.e. 2, 6 and 10, or 3, 7 and 11.

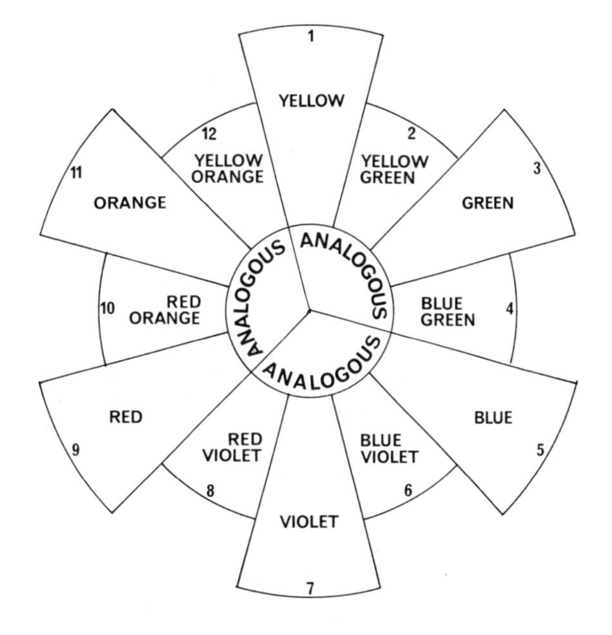

Colour wheel devised by Julia Clements

HINTS FOR JUDGES

The six main principles used in judging flower arrangements are:
Interpretation of the schedule
Design
Colour
Suitability of container to flowers
Condition of plant material
Distinction and originality
Incorporated in the heading of *Design* are sections on balance, scale, harmony and rhythm, for without them there would be no good design. So before a keen flower arranger sets out to be a judge, she must be sure she understands all of the above principles. There is also some advice on judging table arrangements at the end of the section.

The National Association of Flower Arrangement Societies is doing excellent work in the training of judges, organising courses at Area level in order to give teaching and finally to assess the knowledge of judges who wish to go even further, to national level.

In order to help all those wishing to try their skill at judging, and to prepare them for future examinations, I give the following analysis of these main principles.

Interpretation of the Schedule
This means that the exhibit must interpret the wording of the schedule, otherwise it should not be considered further. Even if it is well designed and the flowers perfectly suited to the container, time should not be wasted on it unless the arrangement or composition exemplifies, by its shape, colour, plant material or any other factor, what is demanded of it. For instance, if the class asks for a 'Gay Arrangement for a Dark Hall' and on approaching the exhibits you notice a beautiful arrangement made with mauve scabious, purple dahlias and grey foliage, you should pass it by, even if it is well designed, for you should be able to assess quickly that mauve and purple are not *gay* colours, and also that these *shades* would have no life in a *dark hall.* This is where your knowledge of colour will help.

A knowledge of plant material is also of great value, in fact essential to good judging; it is used in making your first assessment of the exhibits, i.e. interpretation of the schedule. If the class asks for 'An Arrangement in a Basket to Illustrate Autumn Glory', you would be wrong if you gave a prize to an exhibit which featured blue delphiniums, even if it were otherwise perfect, for delphiniums would not be considered interpretative of autumn. Similarly, if a class asks for an 'Arrangement of Leaves, Fruit and Flowers', make sure the exhibit contains all these three items before assessing its value in other respects. So do make sure that the exhibits you will give a second look at really do fully interpret the wording of the class before you go on to other principles.

Design

Design is of great importance. A good design has a pattern, is well scaled, has balance and rhythm. So ask yourself if the exhibit you are judging has a pattern, and do all the stems meet at a unified point? Is this point strengthened with larger or more interesting material for emphasis? Is the fine, sheer material kept to the outside or top of the design and the more dominant placed at the point where all stems meet, which is at the base of the tallest stem? Are there materials used in between the height and depth to give transition? Do your eyes travel from the outside to the centre of interest and rest there, before you consciously assess the other points?

Scale This means that the flowers in the arrangement should be in scale with each other, the arrangement in scale with the vase and the whole composition in scale with the background, space or niche which the exhibitor is allowed. Decide whether the arrangement is the right size for the container. A basic principle is that when judging an upright arrangement the flowers should be at least one-and-a-half times the height of the vase, the width each side often being two thirds of its height. An arrangement in a shallow container can be one-and-a-half times as high as the length of the dish. These are only guides, and in advanced judging much more height is accepted, especially in a shallow-dish design, where so much of the visual weight is low down. Treat the space allowed as a frame: the arrangement should fit into it with space to spare, and be neither too big nor too small.

Balance This means that if you draw an imaginary line down through the centre of the arrangement, each side should appear visually equal. Balance can be symmetric or asymmetric. In the former, the material each side of the axis can be equally distributed, in the latter, one side can be longer, but providing this long swerve is made with *fine* material and is opposed to the other side, which will have shorter, bigger or *heavier* material, it would still appear visually balanced.

Balance can also be obtained with colour. For example, dominant colouring such as lime green and pale pink, if used in large areas on the outside, can over-balance a design, whereas if brought into the centre it could give stabilisation. Test your own assessment of balance by half closing your eyes, then studying the design. Imagine the central line down through the design as being the axis of a see-saw. In a symmetrical style, i.e. triangle, each side can have similar material with strength down the centre and it will appear balanced. In an asymmetrical design you can bring the weight, i.e. heavy leaves or big flowers, nearer in towards the axis on one side, and balance this at the opposing side with long fine sprays. If you assess the visual weights of the material used, it would still appear balanced, just as a man sitting near the centre of a see-saw balances a light child sitting at the end of the opposing side.

Colour

A judge must first consider whether the colour of plant material used in the design fully interprets what is required by the schedule, e.g. yellow is cheerful and gay, blue and violet are subdued, red is exciting, green tranquil and reddish-purple is royal. Some colours are contrasting, such as nos. 1 and 7, or 3 and 9, or 6 and 12, (see colour wheel, page 191), others are analogous; some clash, some harmonise. So it all depends upon what is indicated by the class wording. Colour can express a mood, a situation or an emotion. A class for a 'Gay Cocktail Party' would require some yellow in it, whereas a class expressing the mood 'Dull' would require flowers or leaves of a shaded, greyish variety. Flowers, container and base should be in keeping, although if entering a class for contrasts, the container can contrast with the flowers. White is considered a colour in flower arrangement, but remember it can be too dominant when used as a container for certain flowers. White absorbs colours near to it, black throws the colours back and makes them more brilliant. In a class for 'Variations of One Colour' the flowers, containers and base and/or drapes should all be in keeping. No one can state where one colour starts and another finishes, so the term variations of one colour is often of more assistance when judging than the term 'An Arrangement in any One Colour'. (see Tint, Shade, Variation in definition section).

Suitability of Container to Plant Material

Both in colour, texture and harmony the container should suit the material it holds. Toadstools in silver are incorrect, yet toadstools in moss or wood would be in harmony. A base is considered part of the container, and it can also be the main container providing it holds a water-retaining receptacle above it.

Mrs M. Lee of Whetstone, London, won a first prize with this beautiful wall decoration in a 'golden cascade' class. Against a sea-green background she composed leaves, seed-heads, cones and gourds which was finished with 'bows' of plaintain seed spikes. All then was gilded

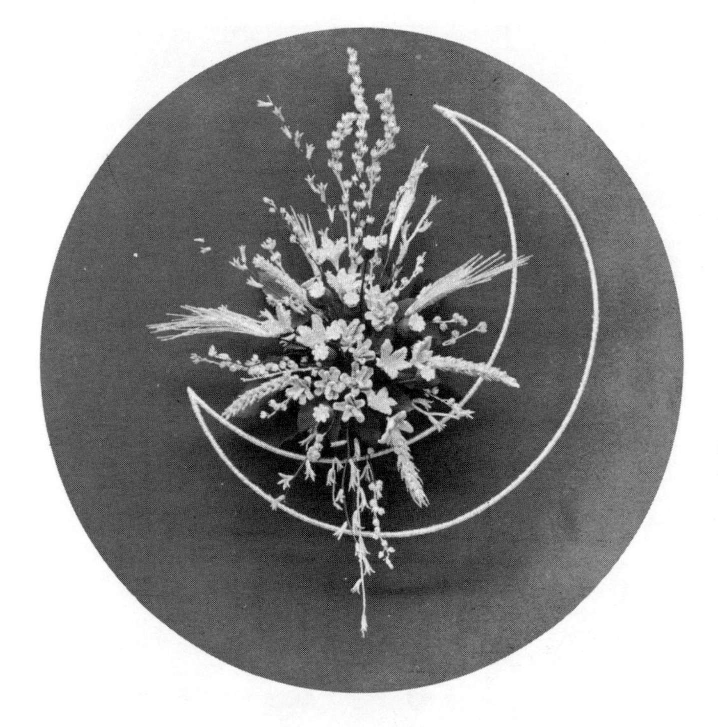

This wall plaque in a 'galaxy' class won a 'best in the show' for Mrs M. Adlam of Balham, London. On an opaque midnight-blue circle, the 'moon' was composed of silver wire. The rest of the material was silvered and glittered, leaves being painted the same colour as the background

This can be a small tin or dish, but once it has been hidden it will be the base which in colour, texture or size will be considered in conjunction with the flowers or plant material used. In period work, a container of the period being portrayed is essential. In upright designs it is better that the container is subservient, otherwise it is easy to have the eye drawn too urgently to the container. Nevertheless, in modern designs the container-cum-base can play an important part in the composition and can take a fair share in the overall design; for in modern work large spaces and contrasts are important.

Condition of Plant Material

If an arrangement possesses plant material which is not fresh then it will immediately lose points. So plants should be in good condition although the stems, blooms and shapes need not be perfect by horticultural standards. There should be no damaged or blemished plant material showing, and wiring is not encouraged. All stems should be in water or water-retaining material. A judge should not interfere with an arrangement unless she thinks the flowers are not in water, but she should have sufficient knowledge of the mechanics of the craft to see whether or not this is the case.

Distinction and Originality

This is a factor in judging that is hard to define. It can be the verve with which some unusual item, colour or container is handled. Whilst originality enters into it, the term must not be used to disguise freakishness. For instance, if some wood-stemmed leaves had been inserted all round the base of a potato and this combination were placed as focal interest, it would constitute something odd, contrived or freakish; whereas if a head of green helleborus were recessed near the wire in the centre at a point where mauve flowers protruded, it would be considered as unusually interesting. Distinction comes with some original thought, some unusual placement or combination of material. It might be an unusual placement in the niche on different-sized bases which counts, or the 'not previously thought of' drape. Any or several of these items will lift one arrangement above the others when all other assessments are equal, and it is a point which is very important in the experience of top judging, for it may not be met lower down the scale.

Judging Table Arrangements

Again the schedule should have been followed. If the schedule states that the arrangement should be on a table which will seat four people, then the size of the arrangement must be taken into consideration. It is generally accepted that the size of the arrangement should be one sixth that of the table, but if only a small table can be provided, the schedule often states that the arrangement can be made to suit a table of, say, six feet long. Consider also whether the schedule states 'A Decorated Table' (in which case the exhibitor can decorate it how she likes and with one or more arrangements), or whether it states a centre-piece or arrangement. Note also whether the use of candles is allowed or whether placements or accessories are allowed, and pass the permitted number only. The colour and texture of the cloth must be considered with the whole, for the entire setting is judged and not just the centre arrangement of flowers. Remember to iron out creases in cloths. Whether the table arrangement is for a luncheon, dinner, tea or a special occasion must also be considered, for gayer, more casual flowers and cloth would be used for luncheons as compared with more formal flowers for dinner, placed perhaps on a satin cloth.

Hints for Judging

After having accepted an invitation to judge, the judge should, on receiving the schedule, read it very carefully. Should there be any ambiguous wording, she should write or phone the show secretary to clarify the position, making sure that the committee, the exhibitors and the judges are all agreed on what is wanted. It is a good idea for a prospective judge to underline any particular points in the wording of the schedule which will have to be considered. For instance if there is a class for a 'Cool Arrangement for a Hot Day', the word 'cool' is the interpretative one and underlining it helps the judge to remember to assess the value of coolness above the other points. Also, should there be a class featuring colours, the prospective judge, by carefully reading the schedule beforehand, is given a chance to familiarise herself with aspects of colouring before she reaches the show-ground.

A judge should arrive on time and be in possession of the schedule; it is bad form to arrive, then ask for a schedule and begin to read it as if for the first time. A judge can contribute by praising the appearance of the show or by making some appreciative remark about it. The committee has usually worked hard, so no goodwill will be earnt by immediately pointing out improvements which could have been made with the staging, etc. These suggestions may be made later when all are relaxed. A judge should greet and be greeted by the show committee, and then ask to be left alone while she assesses the overall standard of the exhibits. A judge is seldom very sociable until after judging is finished, for in judging artistic work she has to tune in to the feeling, mood and interpretation of many exhibitors' work and cannot stop to pass the time of day to all and sundry. A judge should not waste time discussing with co-judges various exhibits which obviously do not conform to the schedule. Nothing is gained by stating how the design could have been improved. This can be done later in the judge's own time, but it must be remembered that secretaries and others are waiting on the judge's decisions, so judging should be concluded as quickly as efficiency allows.

If you are new to judging you might find it a good idea, after greeting the show committee, to walk round all of the classes to assess the overall standard. This allows you to tune in to the quality of the work. Then, on deciding to start to judge a certain class, walk down in front of the exhibits, noting the numbers of any which make an immediate impact on you. Condensed into this first impact will be your knowledge of the six main principles.

Having gathered, shall we say, ten which

appeal to you, I suggest you go over the whole again to ascertain whether in your first enthusiasm you might have missed some which were worthy. You might now have a few more, but it is these exhibits, found on the first two runs, that you begin to judge; the rest you mentally eliminate. If you are one of two or more judges, the others should do the same, conferring all together before making final decisions.

Next try to place the first, second and third prize-winners, but do not appoint them at this stage; check first of all whether they interpret the wording of the class, and check all the other conditions. Then ask yourself how you would reply if your decision were challenged by another competitor. If you can satisfy yourself with reasons and are quite confident you are making the right decision, then, and only then, mark the card. Should you find yourself undecided between what appear as two equally good designs, try starting with a maximum of ten points and take one off for any fault, such as wire showing.

The qualities of a good judge are KNOWLEDGE, FAIRNESS, EXPERIENCE, IMPARTIALITY, COURAGE and TACT, and it is in the interests of all concerned if the judge remains on hand for a while in case of queries.

Judging Japanese Arrangements

Readers might notice that I have refrained from including reference to the judging of Japanese arrangements. I have done this purposely, for when I was in Japan I found that there were no set rules or principles on which these beautiful floral designs could be judged. I witnessed innumerable flower arrangement exhibitions, and although I discovered that some of the work *is* judged or assessed, so much depended on the moods and influences of the day or time, that it was difficult ever to get an exact result. After grasping a principle on which to base my judgment, I learned that there were several exceptions to it; and to try to adapt these principles and exceptions to English standards seems almost impossible.

Schedules in Japan are not drawn up as in Britain, and an arrangement is nearly always a personal expression. Just as it is difficult for us to appreciate the full meaning of a Japanese arrangement, so also it would not be easy for them to understand one of our Easter arrangements which featured perhaps flowers, wood, moss, coloured eggs and a china rabbit. However, rhythmic line, restraint and space should be appreciated, plus a third dimensional effect; and the ends of branches and flowers appear better if they look upwards instead of swerving downwards.

Most Japanese arrangements are seen out of competiton, however, and I am sure that most experienced judges in this country who have widened their minds to all facets of the art of flower arrangement are able to assess in some measure the spiritual beauty of a Japanese arrangement and pass judgement on it if asked to do so in a competition. So I will not confuse you by trying to introduce symbolisms and exceptions to the rules.

THE WORK OF STEWARDS

Stewards play an important role at all flower-arrangement shows. They should therefore fully understand the subject and be conversant with the demands of the schedule, for they are required to be on duty during staging to help exhibitors, and also to be in attendance during judging.

In the U.S.A. no competitor leaves the show room after completing her entry without first checking with a steward to see if she has conformed to the wording of the schedule. Many competitors have the self-discipline to keep their own check, but I have often noticed an exhibitor who is carried away by her creative ability, and continues to add further plants not realising that the final items, which she thought *made* the arrangement, have in fact marred it.

A steward, with the aid of the show secretary, should also be aware of the number of entries in each class and where these are situated, so that she can inform the judge on arrival. She must also know how many prizes or award cards can be presented, for this is often not stated in the schedule. She must also indicate whether there are to be 'best-in-show' awards and be most careful not to turn over any of the prizewinning cards before this has been decided. And, although she often possesses as much knowledge as the judges themselves, she MUST remain unobtrusive during judging and never offer any suggestion. It is hard, I know, but the sensibility of a judge can be completely upset by hearing a comment made by a steward, or her powers of thought can be disturbed by noise and other distractions from stewards.

Only when the class has been *completely* judged should the stewards move forward to affix the appropriate prize labels.

Nothing is more maddening to a judge who, after deciding upon the First and finding herself in the throes of deliberation over the Second and Third, is then accosted by the steward who says - 'I've found the First but where is the Second and Third?'

Judging artistic flower arrangements is no easy matter, and judging interpretative compositions very much harder still. You have only to read the heading on judging to realise what has to be borne in a judge's mind to enable her to assess the qualities of an arrangement; and coupled with that, there is the extra 'emotional' approach that has to be made. A judge has to 'tune in', she requires being left alone in silence. So a member should not accept the position of being a steward if she thinks it entails only the sticking of labels on to cards and listening to the judges' comments.

Stewards can and do contribute a great deal to the success of the judging, which means the success of the show. This is not an easy role to play, especially because it means subduing your own knowledge when you feel you could proffer some help. But stewards should be chosen with care, should possess knowledge and tact, should answer when spoken to without giving anything away (very difficult, this); and if there should be points in the judging which a steward has not understood she can always request a session between stewards and judges at the end of judging. I always welcome it.

HOW TO RUN A FLOWER SHOW

No show could be staged without the exhibitors and no exhibitor would have a chance without the show organising committee. But to make the show a success it must be patronised by members and public alike.

Publicity is of great importance, so tell everyone about your show, announcing it in excited tones firstly to your club members.

Announce your intentions to the local Press, giving them some background stories. Display some posters out in your town, and word them in an appealing manner. 'The Show You Must Not Miss', or 'A Show That Will Interest All Flower Lovers'. Ask your local art school to design some for you.

The schedule, which can also act as a handbill, must be carefully and properly printed, unless the finances of the club will only allow duplicated sheets.

Once the public is at the show every endeavour should be made to keep them interested. A tombola or a raffle could be organised - do display the prizes - and a sales table will increase the takings. Sell plants and other items of interest to the flower-arranger, but do choose sales ladies who can inform and keep all enquiring visitors happy. Do tell visitors who you are. Display a small table giving information on how to join the club, also the date of your next meeting, at which visitors should be welcomed.

Do serve teas, even if this is only a cup of tea and biscuits, as it does avoid the visitor having to leave the hall for refreshment.

An exchange stall is often a good idea. To this members can bring any unwanted vase, gadget, accessory or base, marking it at its lowest value. It can then be exchanged for any other item of similar value.

The attendance of a well-known personality either to open the show or to present the prizes will often attract the public - do remember to mention the fact on your posters! At some larger shows, a showing of slides or a demonstration will certainly interest those who want to know how to do an arrangement themselves. It might even be possible to make an extra charge for this section of the proceedings.

Make every effort to keep those who attend your show happy and interested, and smile and be happy yourself!

Staging the Exhibits

Having decided on the date of your show and booked the hall, it is very necessary to appoint a staging committee composed of enthusiastic, strong members, plus husbands and sons.

Make sure enough tabling is available in the form of trestle tables for the number of entries you expect, or make sure you know where extra tables can be obtained if needed.

HOW TO PLAN YOUR CLUB MEETINGS

Many established flower clubs have become so well organised that they are able to help nearby newly formed groups, but at the same time a number of new clubs spring up which, being far from outside aid, often have difficulty in arranging an interesting programme.

My advice to new chairmen and secretaries is to establish a friendly atmosphere first of all. New members should be introduced to their fellow-members and their capabilities assessed, which can easily be done by organising a showing of the work of, say, twenty members, including the new ones, to be judged by the rest. Secondly, it is not a good idea to get all the best and most famous speakers in the first few months; it is better to reserve them for special occasions, and to use instead the knowledge and ability of talented local members, many of whom have travelled and exhibited round the countryside and really know their subject.

Once it is established that some members have more experience than others, a series of working parties can be organised, where each member makes an arrangement and the more experienced tactfully guide and analyse the work of the novices. All sorts of arguments will arise, but discussion is always good.

An interesting subject for a meeting is for a number of members to set up arrangements for a class title, such as Autumn Glory, and the remaining members to judge by the simple 'three pennies' method. If a 'judge' thinks one exhibit is outstanding, she can place all her three pennies by it, or alternatively she could place two pennies by one and one by another. The exhibitor with the most pennies, of course, wins - and keeps them! Another good idea is for members to bring their own vases and flowers but to exchange them for the duration of the meeting, and to do an arrangement in someone else's vase with their flowers, so testing their own adaptability.

As far as outside help is concerned, local judges will often attend your practice meetings and give advice. For the main monthly meetings, there are many sets of slides that can be borrowed, together with instructive scripts. The area associations of N.A.F.A.S. always have lists of available speakers, and here I would suggest you do not always concentrate on the *arrangement* of flowers. At meetings where there is a competition planned, you could have a speaker on 'Growing Flowers for Decoration' or 'Berry-producing Shrubs'.

Never be afraid to go back to the basic principles of flower arranging for the benefit of beginners. Often potential new members are afraid to make a start at a flower club fearing they do not know enough. It might be announced that a regular afternoon or evening practice class will be held to aid new members. These classes should be conducted by the more experienced members, who will naturally give a warm welcome to the newcomers.

It is up to the committee to travel around to other club meetings, picking up ideas for speakers and subjects. Most areas issue a list of speakers with their specialised subjects which you will find most helpful in planning your programme.

If you wish to know the name and address of the area secretary of your town or district, do write to the Secretary, National Association of Flower Arrangement Societies of Great Britain, at 21 Denbigh Street, London, S.W.1.

Should you wish to join a flower club and are not sure whether one exists in your district, write in the first instance to N.A.F.A.S. at the above address who will advise you of your nearest existing club. If there is not one near to you and you know of other enthusiasts in your district, you might become the prime mover in forming a new club. A small booklet called *Organisation and Management of a Flower Arrangement Society* is available from N.A.F.A.S., and this organisation will give every help.

This mobile seen at a show was composed of perfectly-balanced pieces of driftwood holding dry plant material shaped like flying birds. This exhibit was by Mrs James W. Riley Jnr. of Greenwich

FLOWERS AND LEAVES AND GARDENS

I doubt if there is anything quite as satisfying as having an arrangement of flowers and leaves cut fresh from your own garden. Not everyone, however, who is interested in flower arranging has a garden, in which case a friendly florist and the countryside are your best allies.

It has always seemed a miracle to me that so much can come from so little for, by sowing a few seeds in April or May, you can have beautiful flowers in almost any colour all through summer and autumn. Many leaves are also available from seeds, although I would advise all readers with a garden to plant certain shrubs and trees that will provide greenery all the year round.

Here is a list, obviously not complete, of some of the flowers and plants that I have found interesting, unusual and suitable to grow for decoration. To help those who are not yet gardeners, I have made some abbreviations to help with their method of growing. But the best advice I can give is to make friends with your nearest nurseryman who will advise you on plants, then read a seedsman's catalogue as you would a novel, visualising all the colours and sizes of the items listed and finally, to go to as many flower shows as possible, picking out the plants that interest you. In this way you will quickly learn a lot, although it is rightly said that you never live long enough to know all there is to know about horticulture, for the more you learn the the more you realise you do not know.

I always remember when I first started learning horticulture, for I set myself the task of being able to remember the names of six new plants each day. Then one day during a visit to a famous garden, I walked up to a berrying shrub and said very confidently to the garden owner, 'That's a berberis isn't it?' He, being a noted horticulturalist replied, 'Yes, but which one?' 'Is there another one?' I asked rather crestfallenly. 'Yes,' he added, 'only sixty or more.'

A few pieces picked from the winter garden are here grouped around a piece of driftwood fixed on a pin-holder in a shallow dish on a stand. Height was obtained with grey Stachys lanata *while flowers of ivy and* Viburnum tinus *(laurustinus) were used down the centre. Large bergenia leaves gave weight at the left and the bright orange berries of* Iris foetidissima *can be detected near the grey centaurea leaves*

That was a long time ago, but without going into too many varieties here are my abbreviations for the following list.

H.A. means a hardy annual which can be grown from seed and will die the same year.

H.H.A. means half hardy annual. This needs to be started under heat (in a greenhouse) and put out about June.

H.P. means hardy perennial. These are herbaceous plants, that die down in winter but will grow again each year.

P. means grown mainly from plants obtained from the nurseryman.

Acanthus H.P.: towering spikes of purplish-white flowers, good for drying.

Acroclinium H.A.: various colours; everlasting flowers.

Alchemilla mollis H.P.: lime-green feathery spray of star-like flowers.

Allium H.P.: various colours, grown from bulbs and tubers.

Amaranthus caudatus (love-lies-bleeding) H.H.A.: long red or green tassels.

Artemisia H.H.A.: grey spikes of leaves.

Atriplex hortensis rubra H.A.: maroon-coloured spires of leaves, like wild dock; good for height in large groups.

Begonia rex (indoor plant): variegated leaves.

Bergenia H.P.: large flat leathery leaves, some of which turn a reddish hue in winter.

Canna H.H.A.: maroon and green leaves.

Carrot H.A.: feathery-like leaves for dainty arrangements.

Centaurea ragusina (candissima) H.H.A.: grey leaves.

Chard H.A.: shiny crimson leaves, red veined.

Cineraria maritima (diamond) H.A.: grey leaves.

Cobaea scandens H.H.A.: mauve-green climber (cup-and-saucer-like flower).

Coleus H.H.A.: ornamental leaves of varied colours.

Decorative kale, also Sutton's Glaucous, H.A.: leaves, mauve, green-and-white, green-and-purple.

Euphorbia marginata H.H.A.: green-and-white leaves like flowers.

Fatsia japonica (aralia) shrub: large, glossy, palmate-green leaves.

Fennel H.A.: fluffy, light bottle-green leaves.

Grevillea robusta: green fern-like leaves.

Globe artichoke H.P.: grey-green, large leaves for pedestals.

Hosta (plantain lily) H.P.: large oval ribbed leaves, good for central interest (various varieties).

Onopordum acanthium (cotton thistle) H.P.: grey, large, pinnate leaves.

Ornamental gourds H.A.: hard-surfaced marrow-like fruits (non-edible).

Ornamental sea maize H.A.: striped leaves like aspidistra.

Ricinus sanguineus (castor-oil plant) H.H.A.: maroon, palmate leaves.

Rhodanthe H.A.: pink and white (everlasting flowers).

Salvia argentea H.H.A.: woolly, silvery foliage.

Sidalcea H.P.: tall spires of pink, mauve and white flowers, useful for large summer groups.

Smilax H.P.: long green trails, useful for buffet table and pillar arrangements.

Statice sinuata H.A.: various colours (everlasting flowers).

Verbascum (Sutton's Silver Spires) H.P.: grey, large, velvety leaves.

PLANTS I WOULD NOT BE WITHOUT

Alnus (alder) tree: branches and twigs of catkins so lovely in winter for linear patterns.

Angelica archangelica H.P.: flat light-green heads on tall stems for large groups.

These pristine white flowers of Helleborus niger *(Christmas roses) are here grouped with sprays of* Hamamelis mollis *(witch hazel) in a black container, the right half of which was left free*

Arum italicum H.P.: lovely marbled green leaves appear in winter, then die down in summer.

Astrantia maxima (masterwort) H.P.: pinkish-silver flowers on long stems, which blend well with everything.

Cabbage flower H.A.: round head on tall stem (available from Thompson & Morgan).

Celosia cristata (cockscomb) H.H.A.: has decorative plumes of red and gold, best grown in a greenhouse.

Choisya ternata (mexican orange) shrub: evergreen with white blossom.

Cimicifuga (bugbane) H.P.: tall fine stems of white flowers on blackish stems, good for outlines and table decorations in late summer.

Cleome H.H.A.: Pink Queen and White Queen are two favourites; grows to three feet in height.

Corylopsis (shrub): gives branches of pale-yellow flowers in spring.

Crinum (sometimes called belladonna lilies) hardy bulbs: pink or white lily-like flowers grouped at the top of a thick stem; similar to clivia. They bloom in Autumn.

Echinops H.P.: steely-blue flowers; dries well if picked before maturity; ideal for Christmas designs if flicked with glue and sprinkled with glitter.

Eryngium alpinum (sea holly) H.P.: bluish-white flowers; dries wonderfully.

Euphorbia (Spurge) H.P.: Many varieties; four I love for decorating are *E. polychroma, E. wulfenii, E. griffithii* and *E. marginata.* These are pale acid-green, yellow, orange-brown, leaf-like heads, margined with white, respectively.

Garrya elliptica (silk tassel bush) shrub: long silvery-grey tassels, appearing during January to February; adaptable to any soil.

Hermodactylus tuberosus bulb: dark-green and black mourning widow iris.

Kniphofia (maid of Orleans) H.P.: creamy white, grows to three feet.

Macleaya cordata (plume poppy) H.P.: grows very tall; fine pointed plumes of pinky-beige flowers good for use in large groups.

Molucella laevis (bells of Ireland) H.H.A.: shell-flower on light-green stem which assumes interesting curves; dries well if hung upside down when mature; will also take glycerine and water.

Nicotiana (tobacco flower) H.H.A.: small green flowers on tall stems.

Oxypetalum (tweedia) greenhouse evergreen: pale-blue china-like flowers.

Paeonia delavayi H.P.: small single maroon-coloured blooms.

Pieris japonica (shrub) : evergreen with racemes of white flowers in Spring; looks like lily of the valley.

Phytolacca americana (red-ink plant) H.P.: branching stems of white-green flowers, which later turn to unusual black berries which stain. They are candle-like in appearance.

Schizostylis (Kaffir lily) bulb: pink and red varieties with fine spikes appearing in Autumn.

Scirpus zebrinus P: quill-like stems brightly marked with alternate bands of green and white. A waterside plant, three to four feet high.

Sedum maximum atropurpureum H.P.: long stems of dark-maroon flowers.

Sedum spectabile H.P. : fleshy glaucous greeny-grey leaves with wide head of pink flowers; long-lasting.

Tellima grandiflora H.P.: green, flushed-pink stems of lily of the valley-like flowers; grows up to 2 feet; heart-shaped leaves, which are lovely in autumn.

Zinnia H.H.A.: Green Envy is a green one, and other colours.

Two short stems of this late-flowering Magnolia sinensis *sit well in this antique silver sugar basin on a silver tray*

USEFUL LEAVES FOR DECORATION

Just the right choice of leaf can often add the final touch of beauty to a simple arrangement. But when you are thinking of growing some leaves for yourself, with only limited garden space at your disposal, the decision as to what to grow can become quite acute. To ease the situation, here is a short but by no means complete list of some of the leaves you might find it hardest to do without.

Acanthus: large, shiny green pinnate leaves.
Artemisia: several varieties but *A. ludoviciana* gives 2½ feet stems, of light-grey foliage.
Begonia masoniana (iron cross): grey-green leaves with an 'iron cross' pattern of dull purple in the centre.
Berberis atropurpurea: bushy in growth, giving long arching stems of small purple-maroon leaves.
Bergenia megasea: large, roundish, leathery, glossy leaves.
Convolvulus concorum: shiny, silver-grey leaves; tall, trailing plant.
Cytisus (broom): several varieties, giving long fine spikes.
Elaeagnus aureo-variegata: shiny, golden variegated leaves.
Hedera dentalus aurea (ivy): very decorative yellow and green leaves.
Hosta (funkia): plantain lily, several varieties, with large, ribbed leaves.
Lonicera japonica aureo-reticulata: honey-suckle-like small golden, dappled leaves; a climber, useful for trails.
Lonicera nitida: fine spikes of small green leaves. There is also a yellow variety.
Magnolia grandiflora: large, glossy leaves, brown-felted at the back.
Mahonia aquifolium: large holly-leaved berberis. The leaves turn red in winter.
Paeonia: These leaves are good after flowering has finished.
Pelargonium: foliage varieties give useful leaves.
Pittosporum: several varieties, slightly tender, with small light foliage, good for outlines.
Privet: golden or green leaves; good for linear effects.
Rosemary: silver and green spikes.
Santolina (lavender cotton): stems 2½ feet high, of fine grey spikes.
Senecio cineraria: medium-grey pinnate leaves.
Senecio greyi: grey white-backed leaves, with smooth-edges.
Sorbus aria majestica (whitebeam tree): grey and pale-green foliage.
Verbascum broussa: large grey-white leaves.

WINTER FLOWERS

Those of us with our own gardens always have plenty of flowers for the greater part of the year, but during the later autumn and winter months we are sometimes short of material for cutting. I thought it might be useful to print a list of plants and shrubs which are most useful for this purpose and I sincerely hope that this information may be of value to many of the readers of this book.

Obviously, you will be limited in the number of plants and shrubs you are able to grow, but with a careful choice from this list you should be able to make a selection that will give you a variety of colourful plant material to pick throughout the winter months.

So turn overleaf and choose the winter-flowering plants and shrubs for your garden, whether it be large or small.

These enchanting cyclamen which flower in the spring are casually placed in an ashtray with ivy. Moss held the stems in place

(Page 209) The beautiful blossom of eucryphia which appears in the garden in late summer is here arranged in a pale-pink container trimmed with gold

Hardy Flowers for Cutting During the Winter Months

Period	**Name**	**Colour**
October	*Amarcinum howardii*	pink
October	*Cyclamen europaeum*	rosy crimson
October	*Cyclamen neapolitanum*	pink
October	*Nerine bowdenii*	pink
October and November	Chrysanthemums	various shades
October and November	Roses	various shades
October and November	*Schizostylis coccinea*	red
October and November	*Schizostylis Mrs Hegarty*	pink
October to March	*Viburnum fragrans*	white-tinged pink
November to February	*Rhododendron nobleanum*	red
November to February	*Rhododendron nobleanum album*	white
November to March	*Erica darleyensis*	pink
November to March	*Prunus subhirtella autumnalis*	white-tinged pink
November to April	*Viburnum tinus*	white
December and January	*Garrya elliptica*	green
December and January	*Helleborus niger*	white
December to February	*Arbutus unedo*	white
December to March	*Chimonanthus fragrans*	pale yellow
December to March	*Helleborus corsicus*	pale green
December to March	*Jasminum nudiflorum*	yellow
January and February	*Cyclamen coum*	rosy crimson
January and February	*Hamamelis mollis*	golden yellow
January and February	Snowdrops	white
January to March	*Camellia sasanqua*	rose pink
February	*Berberis japonica*	yellow
February	*Forsythia giraldiana*	yellow
February	*Rhododendron dauricum*	rose purple
February	*Rhododendron moupinense*	white
February	*Rhododendron scabrifolium*	pink
February and March	*Abeliophyllum distichum*	white
February and March	*Amygdalus communis*	pink
February and March	*Amygdalus communis pollardii*	rose pink
February and March	*Amygdalus davidiana alba*	white
February and March	*Camellia J.C. Williams*	pink
February and March	*Camellia oleifera*	white
February and March	*Erica carnea*	various shades
February and March	*Forsythia ovata*	yellow
February and March	*Rhododendron barbatum*	brilliant red
February and March	*Rhododendron lutescens*	yellow
February and March	*Rhododendron rirei*	purple
February and March	*Rhododendron stewartianum*	various colours

Period	Name	Colour
March	*Anemone apennina*	blue
March	*Anemone fulgens*	scarlet
March	*Camellia japonica*	various colours
March	*Corylopsis pauciflora*	pale yellow
March	*Corylopsis spicata*	yellow
March	*Cydonia lagenaria*	red
March	*Erica arborea alpina*	white
March	*Forsythia intermedia spectabilis*	yellow
March	*Leucojum vernum*	white-tipped green
March	*Pieris floribunda*	white
March	*Pieris japonica*	white
March	*Prunus cerasifera blireiana*	bright rose
March	*Prunus conradinae*	pale pink
March	*Prunus yedoensis*	white-tinged pink
March	*Rhododendron cilpinense*	pink
March	*Rhododendron praecox*	rose purple
March	*Rhododendron seta*	pink
March	*Ribes sanguineum splendens*	red

Shrubs with Berries Suitable for Cutting During the Winter Months

Period	Name	Colour
October and November	*Berberis jamesiana*	bright red
October and November	*Berberis rubrostilla*	coral red
October and November	*Berberis subcaulialata*	coral pink
October and November	*Callicarpa giraldiana*	violet
October and November	*Clerodendron trichotomum*	dark blue
October and November	*Euonymus europaeus*	pink
October and November	*Euonymus europaeus fructo albo*	white
October and November	*Euonymus latifolius*	red
October and November	*Euonymus oxyphyllus*	blood red
October and November	*Euonymus planipes*	rosy red
October to December	*Berberis aggregata prattii*	brilliant red
October to December	*Cotoneaster bullata*	brilliant red
October to December	*Cotoneaster dielsiana*	scarlet
October to December	*Viburnum lantana*	red
October to January	*Hippophae rhamnoides*	orange
October to January	*Hymenanthera angustifolia*	white
October to January	*Pyracantha gibbsii*	red
October to January	*Pyracantha gibbsii aurea*	golden yellow
October to January	*Pyracantha rogersiana*	orange
October to January	*Pyracantha rogersiana flava*	yellow
October to January	*Viburnum henryi*	red
October to February	*Cotoneaster rotundifolia*	red
October to February	*Pyracantha angustifolia*	orange yellow

Period	Name	Colour
October to February	*Symphoricarpos racemosus laevigatus*	white
October to March	*Cotoneaster conspicua*	brilliant red
October to March	*Cotoneaster harroviana*	bright red
October to March	*Cotoneaster pannosa*	dark red
October to March	*Pernettya mucronata*	crimson
October to March	*Pernettya mucronata alba*	white
October to March	*Skimmia fortunei*	red
October to March	*Skimmia japonica*	brilliant red
October to March	*Stranvaesia davidiana*	red
October to March	*Stranvaesia undulata*	red

GRASSES

Grasses are an ideal addition to many groupings especially dry arrangements. The following can all be grown from seed:

Agrostis nebulosa (cloud grass): superb.

Briza gracilus (little quaking grass): shakes in the breeze.

Briza maxima : ideal when glittered at Christmas time.

Coix lachryma-jobi (Job's tears): interesting seed-pods.

Eragrostis elegans (love grass): graceful.

Eulalia japonica: long purple panicles.

Gymnothrix latifolia: large nodding spikes.

Hordeum jubatum (squirreltail grass): like a squirrel's furry tail.

Lagurus ovatus (hare's tail grass): as above, but shorter.

Miscanthus sinensis zebrinus: hardy grass, with heads like maize, 6 to 9 feet high.

Pennisetum longistylum: finy, rosy plumes.

Pennisetum ruppelianum: very handsome, with abundant purple spikes.

Stipa pennata (feather grass): 2 feet high.

Zea japonica quadricolor Perfecta: leaves streaked yellow, rose and red.

Zea japonica variegata (variegated maize)

Corn, wheat and oats are also ideal for autumn harvest decorations.

LIST OF SUPPLIERS

Seedsmen

For leaves, gourds, onion-heads and grasses:

Bees Ltd., Corn Exchange, Liverpool 2

Carters Tested Seeds Ltd., Raynes Park, London, S.W.19.

Dobble & Co. Ltd., Edinburgh

Sutton & Sons, Royal Seed Establishment, Reading, Berks.

Thompson & Morgan Ltd., Ipswich, Suffolk

W.J. Unwin Ltd., Histon, Cambs.

Edward Webb & Sons Ltd., Stourbridge, Worcs.

Plantsmen

For leaves from shrubs, trees and plants:

Hillier & Sons, West Hill Nurseries, Winchester, Hants

Geo. Jackman & Sons Ltd., Woking Nurseries, Surrey

R.G. Notcutt Ltd., Woodbridge, Suffolk

L.R. Russell Ltd., Richmond Nurseries, Windlesham, Surrey

Sileve Donard Nurseries, Newcastle, Co. Down, Eire

Waterer & Son & Crisp Ltd., The Floral Mile, Twyford, Berks.

Indoor Plants

Elm Garden Nurseries, Claygate, Surrey

Longmans, Fenchurch Street, London, E.C.3.

Thos. Rochford Ltd., Turnford Hall Nurseries, Broxbourne, Herts.

(Above) Bergenia cordifolia

(Right) Cobaea scandens

Wills & Segar Ltd., Brompton Road, London, S.W.7.

Cacti

Worfield Gardens, Bridgenorth, Salop.

F.M. Court, Moorland Nurseries, Stanley Park, Litherland, Lancs.

Ferns

C. W. Grubb & Sons, Bolton-le-Sands, Carnforth, Lancs.

J. R. Taylor, Lily Hill Nurseries, Bracknell, Berks.

Hazeldene Nursery, Brambridge, Eastleigh, Hants.

SPECIALIST SOCIETIES

National Dahlia Society H. F. Newsom, 93 Byng Road, High Barnet, Herts.
National Chrysanthemum Society S. G. Gosling, 65 St Margaret's Avenue, Whetstone, London, N. 20.
Royal National Rose Society L. G. Turner, Chiswell Green Lane, St Albans, Herts.
National Sweet Pea Society R. J. Huntley, 431 Wokingham Road, Earley, Reading, Berks.
British National Carnation Society E. C. Cook, 1 Evelyn Road, Worthing, Sussex
Iris Society Mrs F. M. Osborn, 144 Ellison Road, London, S.W.16.
Alpine Garden Society E. M. Upward, Room 58, Denison House, 296 Vauxhall Bridge Road, London, S.W.1.
Cactus and Succulent Society of Great Gritain D. V. Brewerton, 26 Chester Road, Seven Kings, Ilford, Essex
British Gladiolus Society J. G. Lord, 25 Kimpton Avenue, Brentwood, Essex
Delphinium Society Dr C. J. H. Topping, 5 Park Lane, Sevenoaks, Kent

GARDENS OPEN TO VIEW

And now, some useful information on gardens open to the public. Try to visit some of them - you will find them interesting, beautiful to look at, and a stimulation to your own ideas on flower growing and arranging.
Royal Botanic Garden, Edinburgh
Famous for its rock garden and collections of rhododendrons, primulas and meconopsis. Open daily all the year. It is accessible by bus from centre of Edinburgh.
University Botanic Garden, Cambridge
It is open daily all the year, except Sundays, and situated off Trumpington Road and easily accessible from the centre of Cambridge.
Savill Garden and Valley Gardens, Windsor Great Park
It is open daily, and is best reached by car from the main London-Virginia Water road and the entrance in Wick Lane: open daily March to October.

Fatsia japonica

Chelsea Show
It is held in the grounds of Royal Hospital, Chelsea, London, S.W.3. from Tuesday to Friday of the third week in May. Admission on the Tuesday is for Fellows and Associates of the Royal Horticultural Society only.
The National Trust
A number of fine gardens are owned by the National Trust and are open to the public. For details apply to 42 Queen Anne's Gate, London, S.W.1.

Hosta crispula

(Above) Arum italicum marmoratum

(Right) Astrantia maxima

National Gardens Scheme

A large number of private gardens are open to the public under the organisation of this scheme. For list of these and times of opening apply to The Secretary, National Gardens Scheme, 57 Lower Belgrave Stree, London, S.W.1. Scotland's Garden Scheme list is obtainable from 26 Castle Terrace, Edinburgh 1.

Gardeners' Sunday

A number of gardens are open to the public in aid of Gardeners' Charities on two Sundays, one during May, the other in June. Lists and details of openings may be obtained from the Organiser, Gardeners' Sunday, White Witches, Claygate Road, Dorking, Surrey.

When to view

As the times at which gardens can be viewed by the public are subject to variation, visitors are advised to contact the Tourist Information Centre of the British Travel Association, 64-65 St James's Street, Piccadilly, London, S.W.1. telephone MAYfair 9191, for up-to-date information.

Euphorbia epithymoides

Tellima grandiflora

Historic Houses, Castles and Gardens
An annual publication from most stationers and bookstalls or direct from Index Publishers, 69 Victoria Street, London, S.W.1. This book will give details about the houses, castles and gardens open to the public, the times when you may view them and information on how to reach them.

Choisya ternata

FLOWER ARRANGING FOR CHILDREN

I've noticed these last few years an increasing interest among children in flower arrangement. I am not referring solely to the summer holiday season when many big town and horticultural society shows include classes for children such as: 'greatest number of wild flowers, a miniature garden, and a decoration on a 6" plate' but to an overall interest which manifests itself in the home, school or at club meetings.

This is possibly due to the fact that young girls now watch their mothers 'doing the flowers' or listen to the discussions at flower arrangement shows or flower club meetings. It could also be because many more books on the subject are now available, but whatever the reasons, I have been deeply gratified to judge children's classes for the Duke of Edinburgh's Award Scheme, and at Young Farmers meetings. Girl Guide club leaders are also including flower arranging in their activities, conscious of the fact that the young girl of today is the proud mother or home-maker of tomorrow.

So whether you are a parent, a teacher, a club leader or a young student, do keep your eyes open for all the wonderful material that grows in gardens or in the countryside which will help you make your very own picture with living flowers.

THE THINGS YOU NEED

There is nothing more enjoyable and satisfying than to create a pleasing picture with a few flowers whether they are picked in the woods, in the garden or by the hedgerows, or even bought from the florist.

We all love flowers yet so often we are confronted with the problem of how best to get them into a vase. Well, please do not be put off, for it is really very easy when you know how and that is exactly what I am going to tell you in this chapter. In fact I believe that after you have read through this only once, you will be able to make a lovely design with living flowers. Yes, it is quite within your power to become an artist very soon, but first of all, as with all hobbies, you

Behind a piece of drift-wood held firmly on a wooden base, pink rose bay willow herb and wild yarrow are placed on a pin-holder in a dish of water. Wild dock was also added low right

will need a few tools. Not many, but just enough to allow you to enjoy arranging your flowers, instead of having to fuss and bother because you cannot find a piece of wire or haven't any scissors with which to cut the stems.

Of course, as you become really interested, I am sure, like me, you will have a special box or drawer in which you can keep all the equipment and odds-and-ends that you will ever need.

But we are only just beginning, and at first all you will want is a container, a word we use to mean any kind of vase or receptacle which will hold water for flowers. Then a holder or some wire to keep your flowers in place, and finally a pair of flower scissors. That is not very much, is it?

Containers

Containers are fascinating things to discover for yourself, and later on in this chapter I will tell you how to make some of these at home, but if you want to make a quick start, I suggest you use either a wineglass, a tin, a plate, a dish, an egg cup or any similar article that will hold water, and make sure that it does not leak.

The photographs in the book show some lovely arrangements you could make in these containers. It is quite exciting to think you could make these yourself after reading just a few pages, even if you have never tried before.

Holders

Holders are most important. So many girls try to manage without them, but it is almost impossible to make a well-designed picture with flowers unless you use some kind of holder to keep the flowers firmly in the place where you put them.

A small piece of crumpled up wire netting gives a grand support when you push it well down into your container and leave about half inch of wire showing above the rim.

If you have a brother who is keen on making things, I am sure a piece of this wire can be found around somewhere, possibly in the garden. If not, I would advise you to pay a visit to the local ironmonger. It is about a shilling a yard. A yard of 2" mesh wire netting is enough for three or four vases, according to the size. Some stores have it already cut.

If you are not sure what size piece will be required to fit your container, try cutting a piece twice the width and twice the height of it, and then press it together until it fits happily inside.

When arranging delicately stemmed flowers such as violets, primroses or snowdrops, you could use a piece of pot cleaner made of wire or plastic mesh. Placed in a glass it gives just the support one needs to hold such fragile flowers in place, and shows them to advantage. Otherwise they fall about and hide each other, which I expect you have noticed.

Another improvisation for a holder is a potato. This is no use, of course, for fine-stemmed flowers, but very useful for holding twigs, small branches and semi-woody stemmed flowers. You should cut the potato lengthwise in half, pressing the flat side down on to the plate or dish which is to hold the arrangement, then inserting the stems into it according to your design. If you find it difficult to push the stems into the potato, try first making a hole with a knitting needle or skewer.

To return to the types of holders which can be used. Some of you may already have one of those glass blocks with holes in them, or a wire-frame type, while possibly those of you who are very fortunate may have one of the pin-type holders. The latter are quite the most

Brown wild dock, plantain leaves, drift-wood and yellow ragwort made this wild flower design in a home-made container

clever of gadgets and are extremely useful, especially when a branch or a few flowers are being used, for they hold the material firmly in place exactly where you put it. You can buy them in a florist's and many departmental stores.

This type of holder, a pin-holder, helps you to make a shaped design, and will greatly aid you if you are creating a scene; in fact I couldn't manage without one. Most clever flower arrangers find that a pin-holder and some wire netting are all they need in the form of holders. (Oasis, a sponge-like block is also excellent).

The main thing is to find a holder, or holders, that you enjoy using - it does not matter what other people like using best - for when you have confidence in your equipment you can do almost anything with flowers.

Flower Scissors

Flower scissors can be bought from a number of shops, or they will order them for you if they are not in stock. They are not expensive, and will prove to be a good investment for they will cut most twigs and heavy stems, and are also invaluable for cutting wire netting for the insides of your vases. They last a very long time with care and you will be more popular if you use these rather then borrow mother's embroidery scissors. You may think you can manage with any kind of scissors, and of course you can in a fashion, but ordinary scissors will only squash the stems of your flowers which prevents them taking in water. So in the end, if you are keen on becoming an artist with flowers, it is better to go without some other amusement or luxury, and buy some real flower arranger's scissors. You might even ask for them as a present when you are due for a gift.

Of course, you are not expected to remember everything after one reading, so I suggest you read through this chapter then try making one of the designs. As you work, you will feel the need to re-read a little, and if you do this each time you try a different design, you will gradually absorb more and more information.

Soon, the day will come when you realise that you remember so much that there is no need even to look at the book. That is the day we all long for, as it is only then you can set about making an arrangement of flowers without thinking of the theory of how to do it. It is at this point in the study of this subject that your creative instinct really begins to show. You will know when it happens for, instead of being bound by rules, you will long to do something because you feel you must express yourself.

HOW DO I START?

First of all you must decide on the shape of your arrangement. In other words, you must have a pattern. Sometimes, the flowers themselves will help you decide which pattern or type of arrangement you will make, at other times, the size or shape of the container will set the note. For instance, a dainty glass vase calls for rather small and delicate flowers whereas a heavy pottery jar would look better if bigger or more common flowers were placed in it.

It is sufficient at this stage, however, for you to know how to make: a triangularly shaped design, a swerved grouping, which is an attractive shape for one end of a table or a mantelshelf, a horizontal design useful for the centre of a table, and an all-round posy for coffee tables, trays and other small tables (see pages 10 and 11).

It will help if you know where the arrangement will eventually stand before you decide upon the shape.

A piece of twisted bleached ivy root was placed on the rim of this grey-white pottery container to make this futuristic design using two white agapanthus blooms and one leaf

Now let us imagine that you are going to make a triangular-shaped display because it is to finally stand on a side-table, backed by the wall. First you crumple up the wire and force it into a vase, making sure that it reaches just above the rim.

Then, with the tallest twigs, leaves, flowers or branches, you make the shape.

Having made the shape or pattern, you start to fill in with slightly shorter flowers by working from the top down to the centre and just over the rim, and from the outside to the inside - near the centre.

As you work down, try not to place any two flowers level with each other, and try to tilt some forward. You may have to cut some of the stems to obtain different heights, but do not worry about this. Place some of the flowers through the wire almost horizontally at a low level, as if they were flowing out over the rim of the vase.

This gives a more artistic finish and unites the flowers with the vase. The final 'filling in' comes with some shorter flowers or leaves, and these are tucked in behind some of the longer bare stems, so that none of the wire is left showing.

If you practise this method several times, you will soon be able to do it. As the seasons change and different flowers gladden us do try and get accustomed to handling them by experimenting with them all; but do remember to place the tallest and pointed ones on the outside to form the shape, and the shortest and biggest blooms nearer the centre, where all the stems should meet.

Of course, you might say that these ideas are all right if you have different kinds of flowers, and you wonder what you would do if you had only a bunch of one kind. Well, if you still decide to make a triangular arrangement, you could follow the same principle, cutting some flowers shorter than the others, placing a few short ones grouped together in the centre.

It may be that it is early spring, and a bunch of six irises have been bought, and as all the stems are the same length you feel quite defeated when you are asked to arrange them.

Do not despair, there is always a way out, and in this case you can find it by very careful cutting, so that, when placed, the irises will make a pattern.

When you use flower like irises, gladioli and similar types, cut them on a slant, just above the point where the leaf joins the stem. This will allow you to place the flower, and afterwards to use the leaves as a background.

Whilst the finished effect looks better if a few leaves are added at the base of the stems, you can try placing some stones at this point, if you happen to live in town and extra leaves are not available.

Stones are great fun to use, for not only do they hide the holders in shallow containers, but they often add unusual interest to a design. Some are delightfully colourful, and if placed low down in a design they accentuate the brilliance of the flowers.

For instance, once I used some mauve-blue irises in a square-shaped dish. In order to hold the flowers in place, I banked them all round with mauve-toned stones which I had picked up on a beach during my summer holidays. A few of the stones had grey and white markings or veins, which, as you can imagine, added even more interest to the colour scheme.

FLOWER ARRANGING IN SCHOOLS

For a number of years I have been deeply interested in helping the young to develop an artistic use of flowers. It is natural for children to want to work with flowers, and

This stabile illustrates both linear rhythm and mass. It has the effect of movement yet is stable (see page 251). The pinks were held in wet Oasis

as young girls are the future home-makers, many schools have already recognised this trend. Some include flower arrangement as an extra subject, and more recently these schools have organised their own shows, staged by parents and teachers.

One school in particular has a rota system of girls who decorate the school premises, each girl on the rota drawing her name out of a hat to discover whether she has to do the flowers for the staircase, the main hall table, the headmistress's room or the art class. This encourages a sense of pride and achievement among the girls, especially since their names are placed beside the exhibit.

To help instruct the girls, some headmistresses call in the help of a member of the local flower club asking her to give a short demonstration to the pupils, and there is nearly always a friend, parent, or flower club member willing to help.

I have spoken in a number of schools, and it has been very rewarding to watch the faces of the girls as they became intrigued with the thought of being able to create a living picture with flowers. Much, of course, depends upon the encouragement they receive from the headmistress and teachers, but there is nearly always a teacher who is very interested in the subject, and it is she who enjoys the reward of a successful show of work on parents' day.

Some time ago I was invited to a girls' school to judge their flower arrangement competition. The exhibits were really lovely and most imaginative. It was obvious that a number of the girls possessed a good understanding of the subject, which was due I found out to the excellent instruction and encouragement given them by their teacher and headmistress.

In one class there were twenty different contributions all made in egg cups, and in another class all the arrangements were made of green material. What an amazing variety of shapes and sizes of green plants and leaves there were to be seen! So many tints and shades of green made the designs all the more interesting. Seed-pods, berries, grasses, leaves, greenish flowers and twigs were all brought into play, which proves that once your mind is set to work on the wording of the competition class (in this case it was 'a green arrangement, featuring any plant material'), your eyes are opened, and you see all kinds of things you hadn't previously thought of using in a 'flower' arrangement.

On this occasion, after judging, I gave a talk and demonstration to the girls, and as I explained the principles of design, I made six different arrangements for them using, for containers, items such as cups, plates, dishes and jelly moulds from the school kitchen.

I looked at the eager faces of the girls before me and thought how lucky they were to have such a lovely subject included in their teaching, for it certainly wasn't included as a domestic subject when I was at school.

At question time, one of the girls who was about twelve years old and obviously very keen, said that she found flower arranging easy when there were lots of flowers about in the garden and fields, but she did not know what to do when there weren't many in the winter-time, and so often it was then that she could not afford to buy any.

This was an intelligent question, and helped me to explain to all the girls how to train their eyes to look for branches, seed-pods, moss, twigs of pine, cones, interesting leaves and barkwood. Almost anything in the plant world, dead or alive, can be used in autumn and winter to make interesting pictures. In looking for this material, I pointed out, it would help if they searched for something tall for the background or height of the design, something such as wild dock, bulrushes, dry grasses or bare twigs, and then to look for material a little bigger in size but shorter in

(Above) This simple arrangement could be achieved by any schoolchild by inserting the daffodils and pussy willow on a pin-holder in a tin of water, covering the tin with wood. Behind the wood add some primroses standing in a small bottle of water. The tiny chicks could be added for Easter time

length for lower down in the design. This might be a piece of bark wood, some large leaves or anything that conforms with the size you need. Then, as focal interest, very low down, you could place some berries, oak apples or cones, or even fungus or stones. But, by the fact that you have used different heights and shapes and sizes, keeping the main interest low down, you are creating an artistic design, instead of just bundling all of these items together in a jar as one used to do.

This suggestion seemed to open up a whole new field of thought, in fact some of the girls said they wished it were winter then so that they could start right away using berries and cones, and all kinds of other unusual material which doesn't strictly come under the heading of flowers.

One of these girls, a few months after my visit, wrote to me saying that previously she had always felt the walk home from school in winter was dull and depressing, but now she was 'seeing' interestingly curved branches, gnarled and twisted pieces of wood, all items that would fit into her designs, whereas formerly she would have thought of them as dead dull branches. She described an arrangement she had made at home from almost nothing, and went on to tell me how delighted her family was with her effort, for previously

(Below) Cowslips are here placed in a pewter mug which was loosely filled with crumpled wire netting. A pewter plate completed the setting

Twigs of pale-green elm were placed with yellow cowslips in this small brown basket suitable for a child to give on Mother's day

they had always referred to her as being clumsy with her hands. Now she felt she was an artist, and I am sure she is.

If you are a parent or teacher encouraging children, try to start them off with some basic ideas. You can suggest they make 'An Arrangement in My Favourite Colour', or 'An Arrangement in a Toy'. Perhaps 'An Arrangement for Teacher's Desk' might be acceptable, and 'An Arrangement Depicting a Pop Record' would be a favourite with teenagers. 'An Arrangement in Anything Which Isn't a Vase' might produce some imaginative results, and 'A Design Representing My Favourite Hobby' is another good idea.

There is nothing more exciting than a flower arrangement show at a school on prizegiving or parents' day, and I have found children much more imaginative in their designs than many adults.

If you are connected with the staging of such shows, do include classes which will give scope for free expression. Classes such as 'An Arrangement Interpreting My Favourite Song' or 'An Arrangement Reminding Me of My Holiday'. You might try 'Sea Treasures' or 'An Arrangement in a Shell', and allow the children to use accessories if they want to. Try to give the less imaginative children something definite to do, such as 'An Arrangement in a Cup and Saucer', 'Accent on One Colour' or 'An All-leaf Arrangement'.

'An Arrangement for a Coffee Table' could also be interesting or 'An Arrangement Including a Bottle'.

HELPING OTHERS

Not long ago, I spent a most interesting afternoon with a group which included club leaders and teachers who were devising a programme that could be followed by the girls during the term. They realised the value of teaching them about the care of plant material and how to cut it, in order not to spoil the parent plant, and agreed that this should be part of the programme.

They all felt that in order to arouse the interest of the girls, a demonstration on how to make a very simple arrangement should be given first of all. This can be done either by the teacher, an experienced club member or by an outside demonstrator. If the girls can see at once how an arrangement is built up, step by step, whether it is in a wine glass or a pie dish, they are immediately anxious to try their own hand at it. Of course, it should be explained that all the stems should meet at one given point in the design, and that this point is emphasized by the placement of stronger or bigger material.

At another lesson it was agreed that they should practise themselves, under the supervision of the teacher or demonstrator, for even at an early stage this practice will show how much they know. Their skill may surprise many, for a number of girls have read a lot and seen a number of shows already but have not had the opportunity to practise.

A third lesson was to be given over to explaining the needs of cut flowers and plant material. It was felt that it was important to help the girls understand that it is best to pick flowers late at night or early morning, and then leave them in a deep bucket of water for some hours or even over night before arranging them. All woody-stemmed material like twigs, shrubs and lilac should be split at the ends to allow for a greater intake of water. Most of the lower leaves should be taken off; for it is the leaves that take up the moisture before it gets to the flower head, and most large leaves should be submerged in water to harden them, which helps them stand up stiffly when arranged. Wild flowers that are drooping need hours of deep drinking before they will revive. White ends of bluebells should be cut off and about two inches of the ends of poppy stems should be first steeped in near boiling water for a few seconds, then placed in ordinary cold water. A little sugar in the water will often help flowers last longer. These lessons or talks were to be followed by practice if they was time.

Another lesson was to be on the value of colours. Blending of colours or near colours such as pale pink, deeper pink, blue-red, maroon-reddish and purple would make an harmonious scheme whereas contrasting colours such as blue and yellow or purple and orange would make a striking effect. When using contrasting colours it was to be explained that a smaller proportion of one colour would be more effective against the other, than if equal proportions of each were used. For instance, if using blue and yellow flowers, it would be preferable to have more yellow flowers on the outside and a few blue ones in the centre, or to reverse this, a greater number of blue ones could be used to form the framework of the design and a few yellow ones in the centre.

A further lesson was to remind them how to pick flowers: never pick too many for their needs, and to cut carefully, not pulling the flowers out by the roots.

Twigs and branches should be cut from behind so that the appearance of the shrubs is not spoiled, or from places where they are unwanted such as extra side shoots. If a twig or branch divides and spreads out, it is best to cut it above a join, as the remaining branch can go on growing in this way. The same applies to roses or other flowers from shrubs. Always cut above a leaf joint, and another stem can then spring forth.

Another lesson was to be given over to the practice of making an arrangement for a special position, such as for 'the coffee table', for 'a country cottage', for 'a blue room', for 'a mantelshelf' and other places in the home.

The lessons were not to be given particularly in this order, but in the order which suited the particular club. For instance, one leader came from the East End of London and knew she would have very little plant material to use. So in her case stress was to be placed on the teaching of design and the use of different shapes and forms, so that when the children went for walks at weekends they could look for suitable items. But one lesson which was certain to be popular in the school clubs was the one on practice for the school show. The girls should be helped and told how to stage their exhibits.

They were to be reminded to plan their arrangements a day or two before and to see that their material is in good condition on the morning of the show. It is better to let them know how much time they will have at their disposal in which to make their designs - they should have at least one hour and of course each one must be given a card on which appears her name, her entry number and the number of the class in which she has entered. This must be placed face downwards, so that the judge does not see it. The show of course should have the appearance and dignity of an important affair. Parents should be invited and if possible a knowledgeable judge should attend, one who can encourage the girls to cooperate with the teachers.

I advised the teachers not to allow the girls, specially the younger ones, to enter for too many classes. It is far better to enter for, shall we say, two classes and to do these with ease, than to be hurried and fussed because five classes have to be completed. Writing of classes reminds me of the importance of following the schedule. For instance, if a class in the schedule calls for an arrangement in an egg cup, this must be used. Just as if the class calls for an arrangement in one colour and two colours are used the arrangement cannot hope to win a prize.

Although it is most important for the girls to follow the schedule, it is just as important, perhaps more so, for it to be worded correctly and by that I mean that there should not be a double meaning to any descriptions of classes. They should be worded so clearly that the girls could only do what was required of them.

Show Schedules

For those who have not yet had the pleasure of seeing a school flower arrangement competition, I print on the next page a copy of the schedule which was drawn up by the organisers of the seventh show staged by a secondary school in the London area.

The girls had been studying flower arrangement for just over two years and had held a show at the end of each term. On this occasion I was invited to judge the exhibits, and they were so good that great credit was due to the teachers and those who had encouraged the competition.

Schedule
Inter-House Flower Arranging Competition

Class 1. Inter-House
An arrangement of flowers suitable for the positions in the school is allocated to each house.
(12 entries in all - 3 entries from each house)

Class 2. Inter-House
A floral composition to advertise any well-

known commodity. Not to exceed 3 ft. over all. (12 entries in all - three from each house)

Class 3. 11 - 12 yrs.
An arrangement of summer flowers. Any container to face front. Not to exceed 2 ft. (26 entries) over all.

Class 4. Open
An arrangement of five blooms with any extra foliage. Not to exceed 2 ft. over all.
(21 entries)

Class 5. Open
A modern line arrangement. Not to exceed 2 ft. over all. (25 entries)

Class 6. Open
A flower arrangement featuring variations of one basic colour. Not to exceed 2 ft.
(9 entries)

Class 7. Open
An arrangement of flowers suitable to take to a patient in hospital. (17 entries)

Class 8. 11 - 12 yrs.
A miniature arrangement. Not to exceed 6 inches over all. (39 entries)

Class 9. Open
A miniature arrangement. Not to exceed 4 inches over all. (64 entries)

The numbers in the brackets represent the numbers of entries that were staged in each class, so by this you can see that at this school the girls fought shy a little of the colour class, whereas they all loved the

Children will enjoy growing these miniature jonquils. Here you see them placed in a small glass vase

miniature classes. The show was staged in the main hall of the school on trestle tables which were covered with white paper. There was also a stand-up background on the tables of off-white corrugated paper curved here and there to form individual niches.

Judging Shows

Teachers often judge the end of term shows and at times journey to other schools to give their help and appear as judges. In order to help those who are new to judging it should be remembered that when contemplating an exhibit, its adherance to the schedule must first of all be established. Providing it comes within the wording of the class in which it is staged, the judge should look for the best combination of the following five principles: (1) design, (2) good colouring, (3) suitability of flowers to the container, (4) freshness and quality of the material, (5) some distinguishing or original factor. The assessment of all of these factors becomes more easy with practice, so I always advise those who have not yet officially tried their hand at judging to observe very carefully all that they see at shows and to try and see by following the schedule how nearly they would agree to the final judgement.

By this it will be seen that you do not judge on what personally appeals to you, for often an arrangement which attracts you because it is perhaps of a colouring or design that you like may not be correct according to the schedule. For instance, when judging the exhibits in class 6 of the schedule on page 230 I was attracted to an arrangement featuring mainly blue flowers but including some white ones. This made it a bi-colour arrangement, and although it was well designed I could not include it in my judgement.

Then again in class 7 some of the designs were really beautiful, but they were not easily transportable and the schedule specifically asked for flowers to be taken to a hospital. I was torn between two very good exhibits in this class. One was made of blue cornflowers placed very artistically in moss in a strawberry chip basket, the other was composed of green grasses and three pink roses and leaves peeping out of the half-closed lid of a small round bon-bon basket. I awarded the first prize to the

An oil funnel, painted white and made watertight is an effective container for a wall decoration. First filled with wire netting, wild flowers were inserted, some flowing downwards. Wet moss or Oasis could also be used to hold the flowers

latter, for not only did it possess a little more distinction than the other, but I felt the blue colouring of the cornflowers would not stand up to artificial lighting, and blue being a cool receding colour it tends to be depressing and therefore is not the wisest choice for a hospital gift. So you see how much has to be taken into consideration when judging, and how easy it is for the uninitiated onlooker to voice his disagreement with the judges.

WILD FLOWERS

Many girls write to tell me of the wild flower competitions for which they enter at country shows and as so many complain that flowers picked in the fields and woods do not last very long, I would like to give you some good news.

They will last quite well if you know how to treat them, for we must remember that once you have cut off the flower from its natural source of nourishment it is inclinded to go limp unless you guard it from wind and warm air, or are able to place it immediately in water.

You see, the wind and sun that absorb the moisture from around the flowers as they grow are normally replaced at once by moisture which travels up the stem from the roots. This cannot happen if you have picked them, but you can help a lot if you wrap your flowers round with paper, right over their heads, or better still with wet newspaper, or take with you a damp cloth which can be placed inside the newspaper. This will help them to live during your return home and once there, it is best to re-cut the stems and plunge them into a deep jug or bucket of water, and leave them in a cool place for some hours or overnight if possible. The big stems should be cut slant-wise, otherwise if they rest flat on the bottom of the receptacle they cannot absorb so much water. Also all large flat leaves and leafy twigs should be completely submerged in water.

The next morning the stems and leaves should be straight and strong, and because they are full of moisture they should last much longer in your decoration.

Plan your design and colour scheme with wild flowers just as you would if you were using garden flowers. Do not fall into the habit of picking anything you see in the hedgerows or woods, but try to have an idea in your mind when you are looking for foliage and flowers.

Just imagine what a pretty arrangement you could make in the summer by using some sprays of green dock at the back for height then placing lovely heads of white cow parsley (or Queen Anne's lace) lower down. Quite near the rim of the vase you could insert green leaves, perhaps of dock or plantain, and in between a few wild, yellow toadflax would look really attractive.

Now when going out to pick, if you had the design I have just described in mind, you would look only for those leaves and flowers, and not pick anything else.

What a charming decoration you could make in the summer with wild foxgloves, or those delightful tall sprays of rose bay willow herb. Both of these are pinkish and could be used for background height. If you combine these with a few purple spear plume thistles, some pale-mauve wild scabious and perhaps blooms of red clover and wild heather, you would have a lovely harmonious colour scheme, which might only be improved by adding perhaps a tiny touch of some yellow flowers near the centre. This idea of adding an unobtrusive touch of yellow to an otherwise monotone arrangement will often give it life, but you try it first and see if you like the effect. If you don't then leave it out, for you are the artist who makes the final decision.

I am becoming excited myself now, thinking of all the dainty wild grasses that grow so freely in our fields, and how perfect they look when arranged with wild oxeye daisies and blue cornflowers in a simple home-made container.

Honeysuckle, too, can be enchanting as a table decoration, with some of the tendrils trailing over the rim of the container and its unforgettable perfume sweetening the air.

You can find wild flowers, leaves and twigs at almost all times of the year in the fields, lanes and woods, and to help you in case you are not familiar with all of this wealth of material at your disposal, I have included a list of wild flowers at the end of this chapter, together with a list of their colours and the times of the year they are flowering. In this way, you can almost make up a scheme at home and then go in search of it, or if you prefer to work the other way round, you can go out, and, after observing what there is available in your district, you can make up your designs on the spot, remembering that you will need different forms and sizes as well as colours. In other words, you will look for flowers, some tall and pointed and some short and more round, or if you are visualising a colour scheme you will search for all pinks and mauves or perhaps flowers coming within the white, yellow and green groups.

You can see how much easier it all becomes if you know what you are looking for. It is much better to be clear in your own mind, than to go out and pick haphazardly, for if you are not clear, it will only worry you and you will not know how to make a good design with what you have gathered once you are home. That is why I always advise my pupils to read and practise as much as they can. The whole subject becomes quite easy after a little practice, and then if you go out with a plan in your mind, you will wonder why previously you were ever bothered about it.

I used to do a lot of practice in trains, and by that I mean mentally planning an arrangement by looking out of the window of the carriage. I do a tremendous lot of travelling every year, and this has helped me to observe what grows in the country, thereby increasing my knowledge of wild flowers. Sometimes I make a note of how many different varieties I have seen on my journey. The best interest of all has come from my playing a game with myself, that of imagining that I can pick anything I see with a view to making an arrangement of it. As the train speeds along, I sometimes decide that I will make a yellow and white scheme, and no matter what else I see growing by the railway banks, I ignore it unless it fits my imaginary design.

On one occasion I looked only for material that would make an all-green design, and I finally decided on tall grasses, some dock leaves and a cluster of green elder berries. Sometimes I change the material I have nearly decided upon, because I see something more suitable, but it's great fun, even making the decision as to what would be best for the occasion.

If I notice flowers that are not familiar to me, I make a note of them stating shape, size and colour and then enquire about them or look up a reference book when I get home. In this way I have learned a great deal, finding it exciting to discover something I never knew before, rather than to go on wondering.

I remember seeing some of the best wild flower arrangements I have ever encountered when I was judging the flower decorations at a flower show in Somerset. Obviously a very high standard of work had already been set by the organisers of the show, as well as by the teachers and the wild flower judges who had given such inspirations and encouragement to the children, for they certainly knew their material and how to handle it.

I recall one arrangement which attracted me for its colour. It was made with tall yellow ragwort and agrimony, with some shorter yellow cat's ears lower down at the side (do you know these flowers, they are so often mistaken for small dandelions?) and then clustered centrally and near the rim of the container were some purple-blue knapweed. These flowers were all held by crumpled wire netting in a vegetable dish with blue and gold markings. The finished design as I saw it was a beautiful thing, and it displayed an aspect of wild flower arranging that I have so often stressed at talks. By that I mean that good colour combination is very essential.

Another arrangement at this show was composed of old man's beard (wild clematis), white oxeye daisies and some of those translucent red wayfarer's berries. Can you visualise how striking this was and how little it would cost if you made it? Yet think of the pleasure it would give all those who saw it. I am sure you will not be able to wait until you can try this for yourself, and quite truly, there is nothing better than practice if you wish to become an artist with flowers.

Because practice is so important, I always encourage my young friends to enter as many competitions as possible, not only at school, but at the big shows that have junior classes and at open classes at fêtes, horticultural and agricultural shows. Show work makes you think, and with the thought of winning a prize, it makes you try just that much harder, which in turn improves your own standard of work. Besides, you learn so much from other competitors.

Also, think how gratifying it is to win in time an award card on which is written 'First', 'Second', 'Third', or even 'Highly Commended' or 'Commended'. If you paste these in a scrapbook, they will always be interesting to look back on. Another idea is to take a note of ideas or flowers and colours that attract you at a show; then you can use these inspirations yourself at some future show.

I was once judging at a show in Cornwall, and in the school children's section I was amazed to learn that there were 334 entries. In this section there were only two classes, one for spring flowers in a jam jar which had to be camouflaged and another for miniature gardens. In judging the spring flower class, the choice of flowers and the skill with which the jars had been camouflaged had to be taken into consideration.

You can imagine what a huge task this was, and how sorry I felt for some of the children, for it was obvious that they could not all win prizes. Still, I know they all enjoyed it. As the children all walked in the tent two by two to stand their exhibits in place, I remember one saying to the other just as they passed me 'I wish we could do this every day, don't you?' And of course, you can, for you can do it every day at home if you wish.

MINIATURE GARDEN ARRANGEMENTS

Miniature garden arrangement is a class which is included in almost all our flower shows, and this is really quite natural since we in Britain are always referred to by people from other countries as a garden-loving nation. Thinking of this and of the popularity of miniature garden making with young people, I feel I should tell you a little more about them, or at least explain a little of what the organisers expect of you if you are to enter your own exhibit into one of these classes at a show.

You are asked to make these to test your skill at design and neatness of execution. Good design in this case means that everything you use in a garden must be in proportion to the size of the box, and by proportion, I mean that if your box is 12 inches by 12 inches, then you must plant very small flowers and trees, and not use large flowers with stems cut down short, hoping this will make them appear small.

For instance, if when out walking you saw a huge chestnut tree, growing in a very small back yard behind a house, you would say that the tree was out of proportion to the size of the garden, and you would be right. Well, this comparison between the size of the miniature garden and what you put in it, is what the judge looks for on the morning of the opening of the show. The same applies not only to small flowers and imitation 'trees' but to all other items you might introduce. You might include in your design a winding path, or a pool of water; perhaps a garden seat or a sun dial. If you do, any of these items should be scaled down to a size that will fit in with the whole garden. Some children include small houses, but I always feel these are not interesting to make in miniature, and I would rather not see them, for after all it is a miniature garden that has to be made and not a house.

So often when judging these classes, I have noticed that most of the gardens are flat, and I am sure if you tried making a garden with a sloping setting sometimes, it would stand out among the rest. You might build up the foundation so that it is high at the left, sloping down over some stones, which would represent boulders, to the centre where you could place a small tin filled with water. Stretching on to the right your garden could become level. At the height on the left, I would place an imitation tree, made from some yew or cupressus or any other greenery you could find in the garden. If it is out of shape, you could even trim it with scissors to look like a miniature tree. Over the stones which will make an uneven but interesting slope, I would place some moss, leaving the tips of the stones showing, and perhaps press in some gravel or sand to represent a path leading down to the pool. The pool, as I have explained, could be a tin lid, but before filling it with water, I think I would fix a few blades of grass to the side of the tin with some Plasticine. I would also press in a few tiny stones and then add the water last.

The blades of grass would then look like tall iris leaves rising from a rocky pool. I might have a path around the pool or make the grass (which, of course, is really moss) come right up to the pool, but I would continue and cover the rest of the garden with moss, inserting perhaps two small beds of tiny flowers. If the right-hand side of the garden came below the level of the box, then I would either insert some sprigs of greenery all round and then clip it with scissors to represent a hedge, or I would paint a white fence inside the box. If you decide on the latter, you should paint it first, in fact I would do it in any case, for even if you decide on the hedge it could be inside the fence and would look very attractive.

If you decide to enter your miniature garden for competition, do remember to see that your garden looks, and is, fresh. Try to work to some colour scheme and keep to it. Do not put too much in your garden; see that it is properly proportioned; and try to make the idea behind the design of your garden very clear to the judge. By that I mean if you visualise a quiet garden where you would go for a quiet retreat, then make it green with trees and perhaps a seat under a rose arbour. If it is to be a busy colourful garden, then have lots of flowers, but plan these well as though you are to be a future landscape gardener, with the tall ones at the back of a border and the short ones in the front. Don't forget the judge will look for (1) good design, (2) a good idea clearly portrayed, (3) good colouring, (4) freshness, (5) no artificial material, and (6) neatness of workmanship. I would even paint the outside of my box to make the whole look like a lovely garden.

Sometimes for a show, you just fill up your box with soil, water it, and trust that it will all last for the duration of the show, but these miniature gardens are delightful in the home and last a long time indoors if you build them up and plant them correctly. I have mentioned boxes, for some shows ask for boxes to be used, others ask for gardens in a plate; sometimes you can use tin lids, but at home you can use anything you like, providing it is shallow.

To make a miniature garden to keep at home, you should first cover the bottom of the dish with small bits of crockery, stones or cinders, and if possible some pieces of charcoal. Charcoal is added to keep the water and soil pure and sweet smelling and it can be obtained at any pet store, ironmongers or chemist. Then cover this with a layer of sand followed by your soil. This should all be pressed down firmly, and of course if you are going to introduce a hillock or a pool, it should be done at this stage.

Press some bigger stones into place with more soil to form the hill. Even the path should be decided upon now for it is difficult to introduce a path once you have covered the whole with moss. You can of course make miniature paths by rolling out very thinly a strip of Plasticine on which you can trace markings which make it look like crazy paving, or of course you can make a path of stepping stones; the ideas are endless. When your garden foundation is nicely and firmly pressed into shape, you can, by using a meat skewer to make holes, insert all kinds of small growing plants, fern seedlings and wild wood flowers, which will continue to grow and delight your eyes for a long time, providing you add some water now and again.

For those who live in flats or in towns and cities there are other ways of having an indoor garden, for lots of plants, pips, seeds and roots will grow indoors even in the winter when its cold outside. The seeds of grapefruit, oranges and lemons make very interesting little trees, and some wonderful indoor gardens can be made from acorns and the roots of vegetables. Gardens also made with pieces collected on a country walk and then planted in a large glass jam jar or a fish or water tank are very interesting to watch develop on your window sill during the long winter months.

But let us learn how to plant pips first. You should soak the seeds or pips in warm water overnight, and then the next morning plant them in a small pot of good soil. You can try four to a pot and you should insert them in the soil about a quarter of an inch deep. If you plant them in summer, the heat from the window and sun will help them to germinate, but in the winter they will need some heat to help them to get started.

In winter stand your pots on a baking tin or biscuit tin lid and keep this on a warm radiator or somewhere where it is warm but not really hot. Of course, when your plants have grown quite a bit and have two leaves each, you will want to transplant them, or separate them, otherwise they will become crowded.

Acorns can be planted 1 inch deep in a little pot on their own. Date stones are great fun to try also, but they need quite a lot of heat to germinate, for they are really natives of the hot desert. Still you can try by planting quite a few, eight or ten, in a fairly large flower pot. Push them down about an inch deep and water them well, and then you should stand them in an airing cupboard or near to some hot pipes or a hot water tank. You should look at them every day to see if they need water and add some if they look dry.

In the beginning they will start to come up like little spikes, very pale yellow, but when they are nearly an inch high you should place them on a sunny window sill. The shoots will then go green and the leaves will start to unfold. The leaves are very decorative, dark green with ridges down them, like the old-fashioned aspidistra. They will go on living for years, as long as you keep them watered.

The roots of vegetables also make lovely

indoor gardens. I have had great fun watching the top of a pineapple grow, and you can try this method with turnips, carrots, swedes and beetroots: in fact try any root vegetable. To make a root garden you prepare a shallow dish, soup plate, tin lid or whatever you may have by placing a layer of clean stones or pebbles on the bottom.

Add a piece of charcoal if you have it (charcoal absorbs poisons, that is why it is added to water for flowers so as to absorb the poisons or bacteria which might be in the water). Then you cut across the vegetable about three inches from the top, but make the thin ones slightly taller and fat ones shorter. You then place the cut end in the dish on the pebbles and place more stones or pebbles around them to keep them in place. You then add water up to the top of the stones.

After some days, the feathery leaves of the carrot will start to appear, the green leaves of the turnip will start to grow and, hoping always that you planted a beetroot that had not already been cooked, you will now also see the lovely red leaves of the beetroot coming up to give colour to the garden.

A little sprig of ivy tucked in between the stones will also continue to grow and add attraction to the 'garden'.

Do remember that although there is a lot of stored nourishment in these roots, and that is why they do not need soil, they do need light, so leave them on a sunny window sill or near the lighted window each day, and also do not forget to add water, so that it is always nearly up to the top of the stones. Do remember that it is very important with these root gardens to have plenty of stones between each root. In fact the roots should not touch each other, otherwise they may rot, and do see that all the stones are clean before using them.

MAKE YOUR OWN CONTAINERS

Half the fun of arranging flowers is to be able to make your own containers, and there are so many novel ways of doing this, that you need never be without something to do the whole year round. 'Let's go out and find something to hold the flowers' is a familiar phrase amongst many young people I know, especially a week or so before the flower show, and some have produced very novel ideas. I think it is the satisfaction of being able to say 'I made it myself' that adds so much to the attraction of entering a flower arrangement in a show set in a home-made container. In fact I always encourage the young people who make these to state on a piece of paper that they have made the container and leave it by their exhibit. A judge always feels that this shows initiative.

Boys usually like fashioning containers from tin and wood, and I have seen some lovely pieces of branch picked up in fields and carved out at a spot to hold water. Knarled branches lend themselves as containers and if a hollow is carved out with a pen knife and then made waterproof by varnish or candlewax, the flowers can then be inserted in this space. You can fill the hollow with wet moss if you like and place the flowers in this, or you might insert a small tin to hold the water.

Cocoa tins can also be cut down about two inches and rolled over to make an edge, in fact quite a number of patterns can be cut to make the rolled-out edges different. Of course you need very sharp wire-cutting scissors to cut the tin and you should be careful not to cut your fingers.

Whilst on the subject of tins, I find that coffee and Golden Syrup tins make ideal containers, this time because the rims turn in. You can make use of this turned-in rim to hold the flowers in place, for if you insert a flower almost horizontally at the right, tucking the end of the stem under the rim at the left, you can obtain a pleasing 'flow' to your design. Of course the tins will look very much better if they are painted.

Square tins are also attractive; in fact mustard and glucose tins remind me of the Chinese pillow vases, and are ideal for modern arrangements.

Shallow luncheon meat tins or dogs' meat tins are also very effective for low table or posy arrangements; in fact a small tin such as this, filled with flowers and then placed on a large tray or plate, can look most unusual.

Shells picked up at the sea side will make most delightful flower containers. You can mount them one on top of the other with the aid of a plaster powder, or you can fix them to pieces of wood with Plasticine so that they will stand firm and straight to hold your flowers. Look for stones and attractively coloured pebbles when you are at the seaside, for all of these items will come in most useful when you are creating winter arrangements.

As you can imagine, there is no end to the ideas for flower containers which can be made at home. Just think how very effective are some of the honey jars and sauce or ketchup bottles, and have you ever tried carving your own container from a piece of soap? I have and it is great fun. You must handle your knife carefully, removing a little soap at a time and, in order to keep the outside firm, I usually start carving from the centre or wherever I require the hollow. I once carved a hole at one end of a tablet of pale-pink soap, and then varnished the interior to make it waterproof and shaped the outside edges. Then finally I filled the opening with grey leaves. Everyone thought the container was composed of some precious oriental stone and were all surprised to learn that it was just soap.

Girls who love knitting and crocheting can make some most unusual flower containers in all kinds of colours, textures and materials.

You can use coloured string, crochet cotton, raffia or wool, and then make a pattern which will cover a glass. When finished, dip the covering in thin glue or stiff starch or strong sugar water and stretch it over the glass. It will then dry the shape of the glass and will adhere for a long time. You leave the glass inside of course to hold the water for the flowers, in fact, you could add a handle to the cover, although if you did this, I would suggest you thread the handle with wire, otherwise it may not keep its shape.

I once saw a very effective container with a handle made by covering a cheap baking tin with plaited raffia, the whole tin being painted with glue which fixed the cover to the tin. The handle, which was wire covered with raffia, was fixed to each side of the tin through a pierced hole. The 'basket' could not have cost more than a few shillings but looked most appealingly different.

Jam jars can be decorated to make very effective containers. You can paint the outsides or the insides so that the colour shines through. A jar could be varnished, and while still sticky, rolled in sand - this gives a very naturalistic effect to the jar.

Another idea is to cover your jar with glue and stick on tiny sea shells, or cover it with bark. With all these ideas you should always have a different-looking container for your flowers.

Once your eyes are opened to all these possibilities, I am sure you will think of many more ideas yourself. In fact you will not in future be able to take a walk in the country, the woods, or along the beach without keeping your eyes open for all kinds of strange or exciting items with which to make a flower container, which in turn will attract the attention of all who see it.

WILD FLOWERS: THEIR COLOUR, SIZE AND SEASON OF FLOWERING

Name of Plant	Colour	Season	Size
Agrimony, Hemp	Pink	Summer & Autumn	3 to 4 ft.
Anemone, Wood	White	Early Spring	4 to 9 ins.
Bear's Garlic	White	Spring & early Summer	6 to 8 ins.
or Ramsons			
Bedstraw, Lady's	Yellow	The whole Summer	6 to 15 ins.
Betony, Wood	Pink	Summer	1 to 2 ft.
Blackberry	Pink	Summer	Trailing
or Bramble			
Bluebell	Blue	Spring	6 to 18 ins.
Borage	Blue	Summer	About 1 ft.
Broom	Yellow	Spring & early Summer	3 to 5 ft.
Bugle	Blue	Spring & early Summer	4 to 12 ins.
Bugloss, Viper's	Blue	All the Summer	1 to 2 ft.
Burnet Saxifrage, Common	White	All the Summer	1 to 2 ft.
Butterbur	Pink	Early Spring	6 ins. to 1 ft.
Buttercup	Yellow	All the Summer	6 ins. to 1 ft.
Campion, Red	Pink	All the Summer	2 to 3 ft.
Campion, White	White	Summer	1 to 2 ft.
Carrot, Wild	White	Summer & Autumn	1 to 3 ft.
Cat's Ear, Long-rooted	Yellow	Summer & Autumn	6 to 18 ins.
Celandine, Lesser	Yellow	Early Spring	Up to 6 ins.
Chamomile, Wild	White	All the Summer	8 to 18 ins.
Charlock	Yellow	All the Summer	1 to 3 ft.
Chicory, Wild	Blue	Summer & Autumn	1 to 3 ft.
or Succory			
Clover, Dutch	White	All the Summer	6 ins. to 1 ft.
Clover, Red	Pink	All the Summer	1 ft. or more
Codlins and Cream	Pinky-mauve	Summer	3 to 4 ft.
Coltsfoot	Yellow	Early Spring	3 to 6 ins.
Corn Cockle	Pink	Summer	2 to 3 ft.
Cornflower	Blue	Summer	About 2 ft.
Cowslip	Yellow	Spring	3 to 6 ins.
Crosswort	Yellow	Spring & early Summer	6 to 18 ins.
Crowfoot, Upright Meadow	Yellow	All the Summer	1 to 3 ft.
Daffodil, Wild	Yellow	Early Spring	2 to 3 ft.
Daisy	White	Nearly all year round	A few inches
Daisy, Oxeye	White	Late Spring & Summer	1 to 2 ft.
Dandelion	Yellow	Throughout the Summer	5 ins. to 1 ft.
Dead-nettle, White	White	Spring to the end of year	6 ins. upwards

Name of Plant	Colour	Season	Size
Devils-bit	Pink	Summer & Autumn	12 to 18 ins.
Dock, Broadleaved	Green tinged with red	Summer & early Autumn	2 to 3 ft.
Dropwort	White	Summer	1 to 2 ft.
Fennel	Yellow	Late Summer & Autumn	2 to 3 ft.
Flag, Yellow	Yellow	Summer	2 ft.
Flax, Common	Blue	Summer	12 to 18 ins.
Fool's Parsley	White	Summer & early Autumn	1 to 2 ft.
Forget-me-not	Blue	Whole Summer	2 to 4 ft.
Foxglove	Pink	Spring & Summer	12 to 18 ins.
Fritillary	White & pink	Spring	1 to 3 ft.
Golden Rod	Yellow	Summer & Autumn	1½ to 2 ft.
Goutweed	White	Summer	6 to 12 ins.
Harebell	Blue	Summer & early Autumn	6 to 18 ins.
Hawkbit	Yellow	Late Summer & Autumn	6 to 18 ins.
Heath, Common	Purple	Summer & Autumn	6 to 18 ins.
Heath, Cross-leaved	Pink	Late Summer	6 ins. to 2 ft.
Heather, or Ling	Purple	Summer	6 to 18 ins.
Hogweed or Cow Parsnip	White	Summer & Autumn	4 to 6 ft.
Honeysuckle	Pink	Summer & Autumn	Trailing
Horehound, Black	Purple	Summer & early Autumn	2 to 3 ft.
Hyacinth, Wild	Blue	Spring	6 to 18 ins.
Ivy	Green	Late Autumn	Trailing
Kingcup or Marsh Marigold	Yellow	Spring & early Summer	About 1 ft.
Knapweed, Black	Pinky-mauve	All Summer	1 to 2 ft.
Lady's Fingers or Kidney Vetch	Yellow	Early Summer	6 to 18 ins.
Lady's Smock	Pink	Spring & early Summer	About 1 ft.
Ling or Heather	Purple	Summer	6 ins. to 2 ft.
Loosestrife, Yellow	Yellow	Summer	2 to 3 ft.
Loosestrife, Purple	Purple	Summer	3 to 5 ft.
Mallow, Musk	Pink	Late Summer	1½ to 2 ft.
Mallow, Common	Pink	Summer	1 to 3 ft.
Marigold, Corn	Yellow	Summer & Autumn	1 ft.
Marigold, Marsh or Kingcup	Yellow	Spring & early Summer	About 1 ft.
Marjoram, Wild	Pink	Summer	1 to 2 ft.
Mayweed, Scentless	White	Summer & Autumn	1 to 1½ ft.
Meadow Crane's-bill	Blue-purple	Summer	2 to 3 ft.
Meadow-Sweet	White	Summer	2 to 3 ft.

Name of Plant	Colour	Season	Size
Old Man's Beard or Traveller's Joy	White	Summer	Trailing
Orchis, Early Purple	Purple	Spring & early Summer	12 to 18 ins.
Orchis, Pyramidal	Purple	Summer	1 ft. or more
Oxlip	Yellow	Early Spring	6 ins. to 1 ft.
Parsnip, Cow	White	Summer & Autumn	4 to 6 ft.
Plantain, Greater	Green	Summer & Autumn	4 to 12 ins.
Plantain, Ribwort	Green	All the Summer	6 to 18 ins.
Poppy, Common Red	Red	All the Summer	1 to 2 ft.
Poppy, Yellow Horned	Yellow	Summer	2 ft.
Primrose	Yellow	Spring	3 to 4 ins.
Ragged Robin	Pink	Spring & Summer	1 to 2 ft.
Ragwort	Yellow	Summer & Autumn	2 to 3 ft.
Ramson's or Bear's Garlic	White	Spring & early Summer	6 to 8 ins.
Rose, Dog	Pink	Early Summer	Trailing
Rose, Field	White	Summer	Trailing
Sage, Wood	Greenish-yellow	Summer & Autumn	1 to 2 ft.
Sainfoin	Pink	Early Summer	12 to 18 ins.
Scabious, Field	Blue	All the Summer	1 to 3 ft.
Self-heal	Blue	Early Summer & Autumn	6 to 12 ins.
Snowdrop	White	Early Spring	4 to 6 ins.
Sorrel, Common	Reddish-green	Summer	1 to 2 ft.
Spurge, Wood	Green	Spring	1 to 2 ft.
Star of Bethlehem, Common	White	Spring & early Summer	4 ins. to 1 ft.
Stitchwort, Greater	White	Spring & early Summer	1 to 2 ft.
Stitchwort, Lesser	White	All the Summer	1 to 2 ft.
Succory or Wild Chicory	Blue	Summer & Autumn	1 to 3 ft.
Tansy	Yellow	End of Summer	2 to 3 ft.
Teasel, Wild	Green turning beige-brown	Autumn	3 to 5 ft.
Thistle, Creeping	Mauve	Summer	2 to 4 ft.
Thistle, Spear	Mauve	Summer & early Autumn	3 to 4 ft.
Thrift	Mauve	Summer	3 to 8 ins.
Thyme, Wild	Mauve	The whole Summer	3 ins. to 1 ft.
Tutsan	Yellow	Summer	1½ to 2 ft.
Vetch, Kidney or Lady's Fingers	Yellow	Early Summer	6 to 8 ins.
Violet, Wood	Violet	Spring & early Summer	6 ins. or more
Willow herb, Rose bay	Pinky-mauve	Summer	3 to 4 ft.
Woundwort	Purple	Summer	2 to 4 ft.
Yarrow	Pink & white	Whole Summer	1 ft.

WILD FLOWERS GROUPED UNDER COLOUR HEADINGS AND WHERE FOUND

White Flowers	Where Found
Anemone, Wood	Woods and copses
Bear's Garlic	Woods, damp shady places
Burnet Saxifrage, Common	Fields, roadsides, dry places
Campion, White	Banks, hedges and cornfields
Clover, Dutch	Meadows and fields
Cow Parsnip or Hogweed	Fields, woods and hedgerows
Daisy	Waysides, fields and lawns
Deed-nettle, White (Does not sting)	Under hedges, grassy roadsides, waste places
Dropwort	Downs, dry fields, chalky places
Fool's Parsley	Fields and roadsides, banks and hedges
Fritillary	Damp fields and meadows
Goutweed	Waste places, near buildings, in damp woods
Hogweed or Cow Parsnip	Fields, woods and hedgerows
Meadow-Sweet	Damp places, water meadows
Old Man's Beard or Traveller's Joy	Hedges, thickets, chalky districts
Oxeye Daisy	Meadows and fields
Ramson's or Bear's Garlic	Woods, damp shady places
Rose, Field	Hedges and thickets
Scentless Mayweed	Waste ground, fields
Snowdrop	Woods and shady places
Star of Bethlehem, Common	Woods and fields
Stitchwort, Greater	Hedgerows, bushy places, open woods
Stitchwort, Lesser	Fields and hedgerows
Traveller's Joy or Old Man's Beard	Hedges, thickets, chalky districts
Wild Carrot	Fields, roadsides and waste places near sea
Wild Chamomile	Fields and waste places

Greenish-white, Green Greenish-yellow Flowers	Where Found
Dock, Broad-leaved	Waste places, roadsides, fields
Greater Plantain	Waste places, roadsides, dry fields
Ivy	On trees, old walls
Ribwort Plantain	Fields, waste places
Teasel, Wild (turns beige-brown)	Roadsides, waste places, copse sides, woods

Yellow Flowers	Where Found
Broom	Commons, heaths, dry places
Buttercup	Almost everywhere
Cat's-ear, Long-rooted	Fields, grassy places
Celandine, Lesser	Waste ground, roadsides, fields, woods and banks
Charlock or Wild Mustard	Cultivated ground
Coltsfoot	Poor ground, waste places, damp or clay soil
Corn Marigold	Cornfields
Cowslip	Open fields, downs
Crosswort	Hedgebanks, copses, shady places
Daffodil, Wild	Meadows and mountain fields
Dandelion	Waste places, roadsides, cultivated ground, fields
Fennel	Coastal districts, cliffs, dry banks near sea
Flag, Yellow	River banks, ditches, marshes
Golden Rod	Woods, hillsides, stony places
Hawkbit, Common	Waste places, fields
Kidney Vetch or Lady's Fingers	Dry fields, hills and stony places
Kingcup or Marsh Marigold	Water Meadows, marshy places and ditches
Lady's Bedstraw	Banks, fields, sandy and dry places
Lady's Fingers or Kidney Vetch	Dry fields, hills and stony places
Marsh Marigold or Kingcup	Water meadows, marshy places and ditches
Oxlip	Copses and chalky meadows
Primrose	Banks, open woods, fields
Ragwort	Dry neglected land, roadsides, waste ground
Sage, Wood	Dry woods, stony banks, thickets
Spurge, Wood	Woods, copses, shady places
Tansy	Waysides, edges of fields, banks of streams
Tutsan	Open woods and thickets
Upright Meadow Crowfoot	Meadows, fields, waste places, cultivated ground
Wild Mustard or Charlock	Cultivated ground
Yellow Horned Poppy	Seashores and sandy places
Yellow Loosestrife	Damp shady places, river banks, marshes

Blue Flowers	Where Found
Bluebell or Wild Hyacinth	Woods, glades, shady places
Borage	Waste ground near buildings
Bugle	Waysides, fields, woods
Cornflower	Cornfields
Devil's-bit	Fields, heaths, meadows
Flax Common	Damp shady places, hedge banks
Forget-me-not	Wet places, by streams and ditches
Harebell	Heaths, dry high fields, banks
Meadow Crane's-Bill	Damp meadow, roadsides
Scabious, Field	Cornfields, waysides, fields

Self-heal	Fields, hedge-banks, waste places
Succory or Wild Chicory	Dry places, roadsides, chalky districts
Violet, Wood	Woods, copses, banks
Viper's Bugloss	Waste ground, chalky or gravelly places
Wild Chicory or Succory	Dry places, roadsides, chalky districts
Wild Hyacinth or Bluebell	Woods, glades, shady places

Red, Shades of Pink or Purple Flowers	**Where Found**
Agrimony, Hemp	Damp places, banks of streams
Betony, Wood	Woods, thickets, hedge banks, grassy places
Blackberry or Bramble	Hedges, thickets, woods and waste places
Butterbur	Damp banks of streams or roadsides
Campion, Red	Damp shady places, hedge banks
Clover, Red	Meadows and hayfields
Codling-and-Cream or Great Willow-herb	Damp places, ditches and low lying ground
Corn Cockle	Cornfields
Foxglove	Roadsides, dry banks, cliffs, woodlands
Fritillary	Chalky places, downs, banks, fields
Heath, Cross-leaved	Moors, commons, damp boggy places, woods
Heather or Ling	Heaths and moors
Honeysuckle	Hedges, thickets, woods
Horehound, Black	Roadsides, waste places, under hedges
Knapweed, Black	Fields and meadows, grassy roadsides, dry places
Knapweed, Great	Fields, waste and chalky places, waysides
Lady's Smock	Damp fields, meadows, sides of streams, moist places
Ling or Heather	Heath and moors
Loosestrife, Purple	Banks of streams, wet places, ditches
Mallow, Common	Waste places, waysides, edges of fields
Mallow, Musk	Hedge banks, dry fields, waysides
Marjoram, Wild	Banks, roadsides, chalky districts
Orchis, Pyramidal	Damp fields and meadows
Poppy, Common Red	Cornfields, waste ground
Ragged Robin	Damp places, ditches, shady places, wet fields
Rose, Dog	Hedges and thickets
Sainfoin	Limestone districts, chalk hills and downs
Sorrel, Common	Fields, waysides
Thistle, Creeping	Cultivated and waste places
Thistle, Spear	Waste ground, fields, commons
Thrift	Rocks, cliffs, sea shores, coastal and hilly places
Thyme, Wild	Dry hill fields, heathlands, downs
Willow-herb, Great or Codling-and-Cream	Damp places, ditches and low lying ground
Woundwort, Hedge	Edges of woods, shady places, foot of banks
Yarrow	Waste ground, fields, roadsides

THE WAY AHEAD

We have advanced so rapidly during the last few years in the art of flower arrangement that many, ever anxious to rush on to new creativity, are alrady asking what the next move is. Sometimes we try something new only to return to what we know and understand, but we will always seek after the new, for art will always progress.

The reason for this rapid development of ideas might have been occasioned by the tremendous appeal that our major flower arrangement shows have on the imaginations of the public. The organizers of these shows, in their turn, realize that a change must be offered or something new presented in order to attract the public.

Many of us have witnessed the revolution in painting and other forms of art, where many not satisfied with the modern styles of expression have rushed into excess and have given us Abstract, Cubism, and Surrealism. Exhibits, portraying these 'isms', are given much space in galleries and shown to the public, yet few, let alone the artists, can explain them. As one abstract artist said to me: 'You do not interpret, it *is* something not *about* something'.

During my travels, especially in Japan and the U.S.A., I have witnessed, discussed and even practised some of the new trends in flower arrangement, such as Abstract, Realistic and non-Realistic, Futurism and Impressionism. In arts other than flower arranging this latter can be manifested by 'action' music with silent instruments played in total silence, or a huge square canvas can be painted totally in black - it being said that if you look long enough you can see other colours - but apart from listening to talks on this, I have yet to see a flower arrangement portraying the value of nothingness. However, it might come yet.

This chapter is not easy to write, for although I am forever looking forward, seeking or sensing the new, giving a lead

Angles and spaces, twists and turns are all part of the way ahead in future flower arranging. Here curls of bleached broom (sprayed with grey paint) are fixed on a pin-holder in an antique Etruscan vase. The lotus seed-heads, similarly painted, are tied and grouped close together, the vase being filled with grey stone chips. Further stone chips are added to the black lacquered bases

to those who quickly tire of just 'doing the flowers', I find I am not altogether in agreement with many of the styles that are being termed 'new'.

I find them arresting and am always attracted when I see them displayed in illuminated niches at a show, but I am not sure they were ever intended as decorations for the home. However, as flower arranging is an expressive art, I am sure many find these new styles interesting because they distract, and perhaps in many modern settings they are required to do just that.

Not all of the new ideas now being practised in flower arranging can be grouped together under one heading, such as Abstract, although many of the surrealistic and impressionistic designs could also be classed as abstract, but one factor that is recognisable in all these 'new' designs is the emphasis on form.

ABSTRACT

Space and form in abstract arrangements are very important, for when creating such an arrangement you are not *adding* items to make your arrangement, you are *taking away*. The space left has therefore great value, for the eye of the abstract arranger sees her arrangement before it formed spaces i.e. she visualised the pattern of the arrangement before she abstracted some items. Abstract arrangements are two dimensional and they are non-recognisable - in other words, they do not have to represent anything. The arranger is placing forms within space in a two dimensional manner. Neither is any emotion expressed in an abstract arrangement; in fact, to assess such a design much more freedom must be allowed when thinking of many of the accepted principles - principles such as scale, balance, rhythm, unity and texture.

For instance, a line need not be rhythmic, nor need there be any visible transition, for

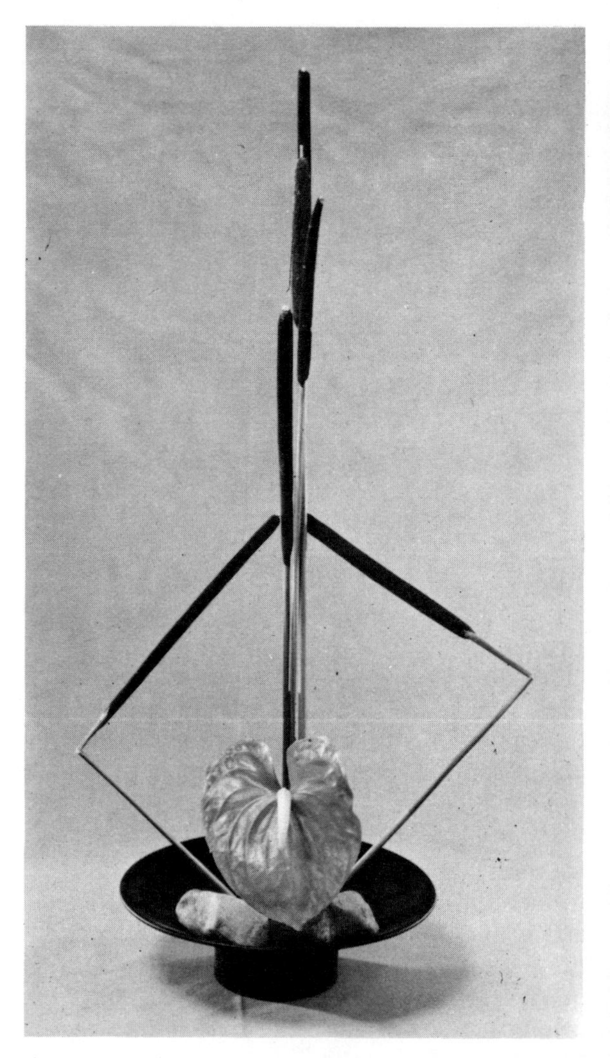

(Above) This is an abstract design in its simplest form. The red anthurium is shown within the enclosed space made by bent bulrushes, while more bulrushes give height. Note the contrast of form; try to envisage that this might have been a low triangular mass design before parts were extracted

(Right) In this modern pottery double-opening container by Anschel of Chelsea, bleached broom was placed to form enclosed spaces. Two pink anthuriums and a leaf filled the central space, and the empty neck of the container gave solid form to the low right space

The three 'flowers' placed on top of a Redland garden tile are made from dried orange peel. Slit the peel down in six parts within an inch or two of the stem end. Take out the fruit and dry over a cup or small glass. The centres are lily seed-pods pushed through on to a wire stem. A dry, pale-green cycas leaf flows over the bareness of the tile

perhaps the arranger could see rhythmic lines and transition before they were abstracted.

Abstract arrangements are usually taller than the accepted balanced height, they depict strong contrast in colour and in texture or material, not all of which need be plant material, and certainly no whimsical figurines or sentimental accessories are used.

MOBILES AND STABILES

We have already seen a few mobile exhibits in our shows and almost certainly we shall have stabiles (stable mobiles). Whereas a hanging mobile is composed of various objects so grouped that they have the *quality* of movement, in fact, the actual mobile often moves with the slightest stir in the air; while a stabile is a combination of line and mass to make a non-moving composition, although it appears as though it would move.

EXPRESSIONISM

Expressionist arrangements emphasise emotions and inner sensations such as fear or joy, rather than conveying a solid form. The arranger can therefore distort in colour or shape or size in order to convey meaning.

OBJECTIVITY

Objective arrangements portray flowers, plants and all items with no desire to distort or to alter the form or colour when seen by someone else. The arrangement could be idealistic or dramatised by shapes or colours, but the object expressed in the arrangement is always clearly recognized.

One dozen red carnations are here clustered at the base of four swirls of dry broom painted white. All are held in a Universal bowl on top of the tall narrow-necked vase

REALISM AND NON-REALISM

Realistic arrangements are portrayed with great fidelity of plant material, whereas in non-realistic arrangements items such as springs, junk objects and other non-plant material may be included, providing it has form and visual attraction, perhaps of surface texture.

As I recall viewing many of these new-type arrangements, most of which I could not understand, I was told that if I found them difficult to understand it might be a shortcoming within me. I must keep an open mind, I was told, and try to accept new experiments and expressions; in fact, one should give the 'new' arranger the same encouragement that is generously accorded to experimental scientists.

On this note I am reminded that about fifteen years ago, any modern-styled arrangement I made of roses with wood was immediately decried, it being said that roses could not possibly be arranged in such a manner; that they had to be massed in a silver or glass bowl.

So, with mind wide open, I continue to experiment, realising that what is new today may be fully accepted, even surpassed, in ten years time.

INDEX

Abbreviation : p = photograph or illustration